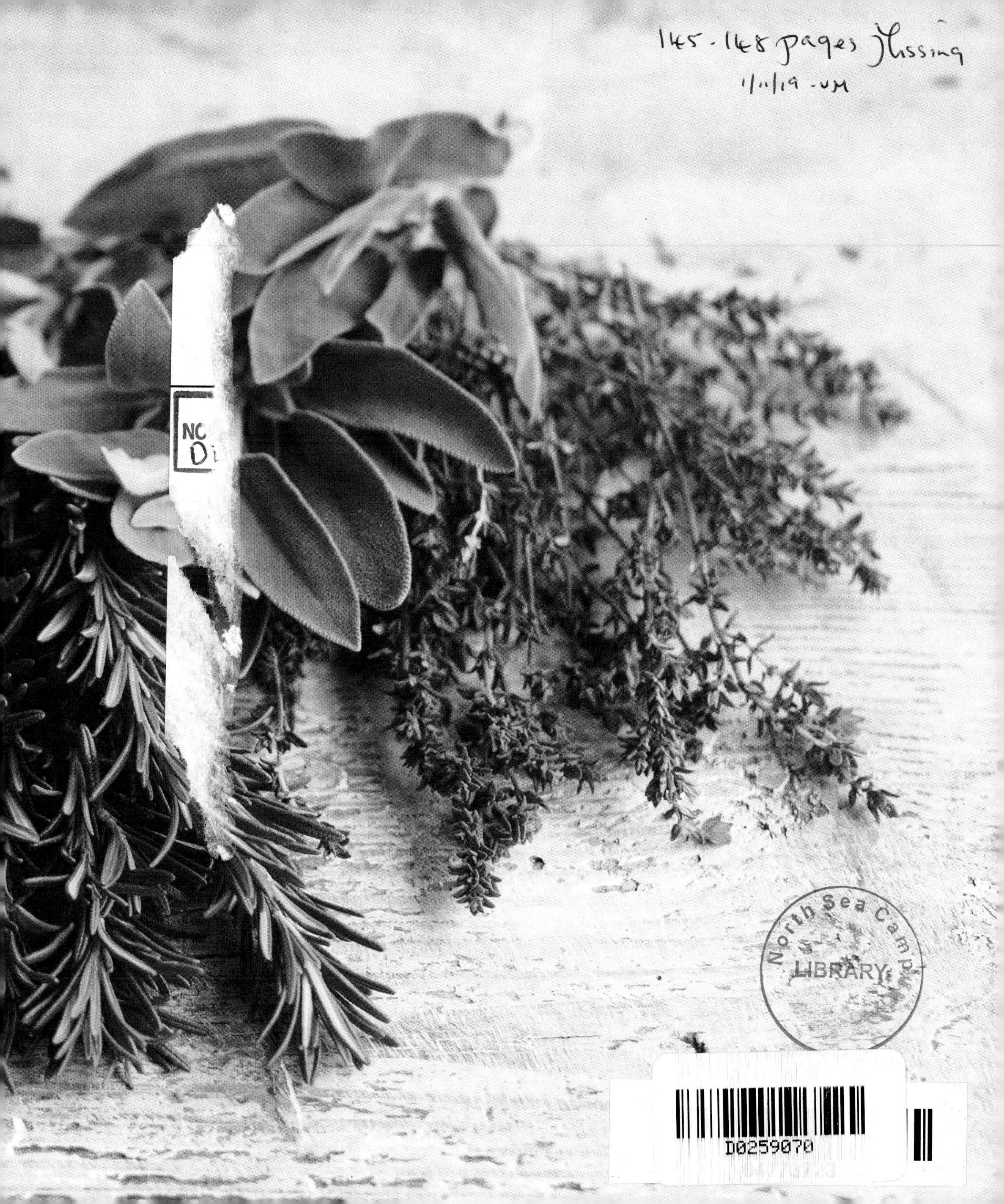

sausages

sausages

paul gayler

jacqui
small

First published in 2011 by
Jacqui Small LLP
An imprint of Aurum Books
7 Greenland Street
London NW1 OND

Text copyright © Paul Gayler 2011
Design and layout copyright
© Jacqui Small 2011

Publisher: **Jacqui Small**
Managing Editor: **Kerenza Swift**
Art Director: **Penny Stock**
Editor: **Hilary Mandleberg**
Production: **Peter Colley**

ISBN 978 1 906417 58 1

A catalogue record for this book is available
from the British Library.

2013 2012 2011

10 9 8 7 6 5 4 3 2 1

Printed in **Singapore**

contents

introduction

I suppose my love of sausages started when I was a child. We often ate sausages at home; they were cheap and filling, as well as versatile and quick to prepare. My mother would cook them in all sorts of tasty ways, from fried sausages as part of a traditional British breakfast, to 'bangers and mash' and 'toad in the hole'. On Bonfire Night we'd simply put a sausage on the end of a long stick and cook it in the dying embers of the bonfire. At weekends, I'd be at a football match with Dad and we'd have a 'hot dog' treat at half time.

Sausages are one of the world's great comfort foods, but they've come a long way since my childhood. With the rise of specialist butchers, delis, online offers and the vast improvement of supermarket varieties, there has never been a better time to buy a sausage that will appeal to you, whether you prefer traditional recipes or experimental ones.

The sausage, which was once nothing more than a mid-week staple, has now even taken on 'designer' status with many of the premium sausage makers using rare-breed organic pork from pigs such as the Gloucester Old Spot, the Middle White, the Berkshire and the Tamworth.

Despite the extra cost of such sausages, the British sausage industry is in its best shape for years and most of the recent growth comes from premium-range varieties. We British now eat around 250,000 tonnes of sausages a year, which equates to around 5 million a day.

So what are the sausages that are on offer? As well as the great British classics like the peppery Cumberland that is traditionally made in a coil shape, or the Lincolnshire, made with sage, there is a whole world of sausages out there. With offerings from Europe, North and South America, North and South Africa and Asia, as well as Australia and New Zealand, it would take months of sausage eating to get through them all.

And that's not the whole story. As well as vegetarian sausages and gluten-free varieties, many contemporary sausages are now widely on sale. A quick glance at a good deli counter reveals sausages made with chilli, with red onion, with buffalo meat, with sour cherries – the list goes on.

Unfortunately, cheap mass-produced sausages made from mechanically recovered meat laden with cereal, standardised seasonings and preservatives, and encased in edible plastic skins are still with us. Not surprisingly, I suggest you give these a wide berth. Once you've tasted the real thing, you'll know why.

Which leads me to this book. In it you'll discover exactly what makes a great sausage and you'll learn about many of the different types worldwide (I can't possibly name them all so I've chosen examples of what I believe to be most popular) and their classifications. I've also included a short history of sausage-making and some fun and interesting sausage facts.

If you've ever had the urge to make your own sausages, it's not as daunting as you may think. As well as giving you 16 key recipes for my favourite sausages, I'll show you how to make them step by step, either with equipment you've already got at home or, if you want to go the whole hog (excuse the pun!), using specialist sausage-making kit.

And last but by no means least, there are seven chapters offering nearly 90 mouthwatering recipes involving more than 40 different types of sausages, plus a chapter of simple and delicious sauces and relishes that are unbeatable with simple grilled, barbecued, fried or baked sausages.

I hope this book will inspire you to make your own sausages but if you decide this is a step too far, be assured you'll find great-tasting sausages at good deli counters, at African, Asian and Eastern European grocers, and at your nearest specialist butcher – where you may well find delicious locally made sausages.

Whichever sausages you opt for, I wish you happy eating.

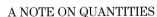

A NOTE ON QUANTITIES
Most of the recipes in this book are for 4 servings and call for 8–12 sausages per four people or, in some instances, 450–500g (14½oz–1lb) of sausages. If you've got an average appetite, you'll be happy eating two sausages, but if you've got a healthier appetite like me, three will be better. Remember – sausages can be moreish.
Note: Both metric and imperial measurements are used in the recipes. You should use one system or the other; do not attempt to mix them.

the story of
sausages

a short history of the sausage

The stories of how and where sausages originated are many and contradictory but it is thought that the first sausages were made of roasted intestines mixed with fat and salt. The Greek poet Homer mentions a type of blood sausage in his book *The Odyssey*, written some 2700 years ago, but evidence shows that even by then, sausages were already popular throughout Greece and Italy.

This must surely mean that sausages are one of the oldest processed convenience foods known to humankind. What is more, butchers must have quickly realised their value. Sausages were an extremely economical – if not always appealing – way of making use of the whole animal, from the meat to the organs to the fat. And to cap it all, they were nutritious as well.

It would appear that there have always been two distinct types of sausage – those that were preserved in salt and dried (the word 'sausage' is derived from the Latin word *salsus*, meaning 'salted' or 'preserved') and fresh sausages that were cooked and eaten immediately.

Although salt was used to preserve sausages, other methods such as drying, curing, smoking or a mix of several techniques were also common. Clearly, being able to preserve sausages was especially useful before the days of refrigeration.

Fresh sausages have been made for as long as cured ones. The first fresh sausages, made just from minced meat and fat, were similar to patties or burgers. Later, the Romans added spices such as cumin, bay leaf and black pepper for extra flavour. Other exotic spices and seasonings were introduced when travellers brought them back from their journeys in the Middle East, the New World and the Indies.

What the Romans did for us

Sausages in the shape and form we know them today were first invented by the Romans. It was they who developed the art of stuffing coarsely minced pork or pork mixed with other meats, fat and seasonings into skins or casings. These sausages were an overnight success and quickly became the most popular festival and fairground food. It wasn't long before they became associated with the wild feast of Lupercalia, with the result that Emperor Constantine the Great attempted to ban them on the grounds that they were ruining public morals. Fortunately he did not succeed!

Every country that came under Roman sway enthused over Roman sausages and began copying them. It is believed, for example, that sausages were first brought to Britain by the Romans some time before 400AD.

After the fall of the Roman Empire, people all over Europe went on making sausages in the Roman style and still do so to this day. Italian mortadella and some German sausages have scarcely changed since Roman times.

Later developments

Although pork was the first meat used to make sausages, other meats were introduced later. These included beef, veal, mutton and venison. The addition of dried blood produced the black pudding. Over time, different countries developed their own distinct style of sausages, using both local ingredients (sage for Lincolnshire sausages and apples for Somerset sausages being just two English examples) and imported spices and flavourings.

Nowadays, many of the world's best-loved sausages are named after the locality where they were first made. Think of the frankfurter from Frankfurt and bologna from Bologna.

Thanks to the development of good transport links worldwide, it is now possible to buy many foreign varieties of sausage, especially if you have the advantage of living in a large cosmopolitan city.

But if you prefer the idea of making your own, then you are not alone. Many people are turning to sausage-making at home, whether out of concern for animal welfare or to avoid the cheap mass-produced sausages of the supermarkets.

some sausage facts

- Sausages are an excellent source of protein, containing all the essential amino acids necessary for growth.

- Premium sausages generally have natural casings, or skins, made from the intestines of pigs (hogs) or sheep. Cheaper sausages have casings made from re-formed collagen and cellulose.

- Sausages should be cooked slowly over a medium heat. They definitely should not be pricked with a fork. If you prick them, they are more likely to burst and then you will lose all the flavourful juices.

- The most expensive sausage ever was made using fillet steak combined with champagne and Périgord truffles.

- The world's longest sausage was made in England. It was 56km (35 miles) long.

- The nickname 'bangers' was first given to sausages during World War I, when the sausages exploded in the pan while being cooked. It was a time of meat rationing, so manufacturers bulked the sausages up with cereal and water. The sausages exploded during cooking because the water turned to steam.

- Americans eat 7 billion hot dogs between Memorial Day and Labour Day alone. That's 50,000,000 a week for 14 weeks! And hot dog vendors at baseball games reputedly each sell 12,000 hot dogs per season.

- Germany, the home of over 1500 varieties of sausage, now offers a diploma in the art of sausages. It is taught at the Sausage Academy in Neumarkt.

- Statistics show that 90 per cent of British households buy sausages, enjoying them for breakfast, lunch, evening suppers, barbecues and to include in children's school lunch boxes. Traditional country pork sausages are the British favourite, closely followed by beef.

- The English highwayman Dick Turpin was known to moonlight as a butcher, making sausages from animals that were hunted in Epping Forest.

- Celebrity fans of the sausage include Michael Caine, Roger Moore and the late Elizabeth Taylor. She was said to always enjoy 'bangers and mash' when she visited London. Footballer John Terry and his wife had a wedding breakfast of bangers and mash, while Katie Price and Peter André, as well as Kate Winslet, were also served bangers and mash at their weddings.

the variety of sausages

According to Wikipedia, a sausage is a food consisting of minced meat mixed with seasonings and usually formed in a casing. Every nation has its sausages but they are all made in roughly this way.

Throughout most of the European Union, sausages are made from a blend of pork and beef, pork and veal or sometimes from ham and bacon, while in Britain, most sausages are generally made from one meat, namely pork. British sausages are mostly fresh (see below) and have a crumbly texture, but the texture of other European sausages can vary: in some the meat is minced as finely as in pâté, while in others the meat is coarsely ground. In some European sausages the meat mixture is studded with small pieces of meat or fat, which gives a speckled appearance to the sausage when it is thinly sliced.

The USA imports most European sausages and makes its own variations of them, but the most popular home-made varieties are the regional ones, like Cajun andouille (see page 33). Some imports go by different names, so mortadella is known as bologna in the USA.

Sausage classification

It can be bewildering to be confronted by row upon row of sausages in butchers shops and delis, especially when their classifications vary from country to country and their names can be long and foreign-sounding. The following are the generally accepted classifications.

FRESH SAUSAGES

Fresh sausages are made with fresh meat such as pork, veal, beef or chicken. You can keep them in the fridge for four to five days and you can freeze them for up to three months.

Fresh sausages must be thoroughly cooked through just before you serve them.

If you prefer, you can make fresh sausage mix into patties and meatballs instead of putting it into traditional casings.

Examples of fresh sausages are varieties such as country pork (see page 14, number 4) – the traditional English 'banger' – Cumberland (see page 14, number 13), Oxford (see page 15, number 17) and Lincolnshire (see page 14, number 2). Looking further afield, Italian luganega (see page 15, number 1), French Toulouse (see page 14, number 10) and South African boerewors (see page 14, number 16) are other examples of fresh sausages.

PRE-COOKED SAUSAGES

These sausages are made with fresh meat that is cooked or partially cooked as part of the making process. The cooking can involve smoking, steaming or poaching. Some pre-cooked sausages are smoked as well as steamed or poached to give them extra flavour.

Pre-cooked sausages are generally fried or grilled before serving. Examples of these sausages are German Bratwurst (see page 14, number 7), French white pudding, or boudin blanc (see page 14, number 14), saveloys (see page 15, number 16) and frankfurters (hot dogs).

Smoked varieties include kielbasa, kabanos (see page 15, number 6), chorizo and mortadella (see page 15, number 9). These can be eaten hot or cold.

SEMI-DRIED AND DRIED SAUSAGES

Sausages can be semi- or fully dried in controlled conditions over a period of months as a way of preserving them. Once they have been dried, they can also be smoked.

This group of sausages includes salami and cured chorizo. They can all be stored, unrefrigerated, for months without deterioration. In fact, in America, dried sausage is often referred to as 'summer sausage' because it does not need to be kept in the fridge during warm weather. These semi-dried and dried sausages are generally eaten as they are – usually thinly sliced – but they can also be used to great effect in cooking.

my favourite sausages

Everyone has their personal favourite sausage, often depending on where you live. It is estimated that there are around 4500 varieties worldwide, with 1500 in Germany alone and, according to the British Sausage Appreciation Society, over 400 varieties in Britain.

The market for sausages is always growing. People love the traditional varieties but modern sausage makers are always trying to entice the public to buy more by offering new flavourings and seasonings.

On pages 16–19 you will find a selection of my favourite sausages. The first two pages show some of the huge variety of sausages you can make yourself. I give all the recipes for these on pages 30–41. Pages 18–19 show my favourite sausages to buy. You can find these at butchers, specialist delis and supermarkets as well as via the internet. Some, it is fair to say, are easier to obtain than others, but they are all well worth the effort.

Sausages to make

1 Loukanika A traditional Greek sausage made from pork or lamb and often distinctively flavoured with the addition of Greek wine, spices and finely grated orange zest. It must be cooked before eating.

2 Lincolnshire A regional British sausage, made from pork flavoured with sage.

3 Faggots A traditional patty-style pork sausage made from pork, pork offal, spices and herbs and wrapped in pig's caul (crépine). It is delicious with mashed potatoes, cabbage and onion gravy.

4 Country pork This best-selling traditional mild-flavoured sausage is Britain's much-vaunted 'banger'. It is known by a variety of names such as 'traditional' or 'farmhouse', with each recipe varying according to the butcher or manufacturer. When you have a traditional English breakfast, bangers and mash or toad-in-the-hole, then you will be eating country pork sausages. They are an all-round winner. What is more, if you are making your own (see p.30), you can produce many variations from the basic recipe.

5 Cajun andouille This spicy sausage should not be confused with French andouillette, which is made from pigs' intestines and is regarded by many as something of an acquired taste. Cajun andouille is smoked over wood chips. My version is unsmoked but is delicious all the same. This sausage is great in jambalaya and gumbos.

6 Chorizo picante A Spanish and Mexican sausage made from pork with lots of spices, including smoked paprika (pimentón), this is not to be confused with cured chorizo (see opposite). Cook this as you would cook any fresh sausage. It is great with fish and shellfish, especially oysters and scallops, and is often served as part of a tapas selection.

7 Bratwurst From the German *Brat*, meaning finely chopped meat and *Wurst* meaning sausage, Bratwurst is a pre-cooked German sausage made from a blend of pork and veal flavoured with onion and subtle spices. It needs to be cooked before eating. Bratwurst is great the German way – grilled or simmered in beer and served with sauerkraut.

8 Bockwurst Bockwurst is one of Germany's most popular sausages but is also a favourite in the USA and other parts of the world. Made from veal and pork, it is very tasty served hot with sauerkraut or with potato salad.

9 Venison This gourmet speciality sausage is both extremely tasty and low in fat. It can be made with other game as well as with venison. All venison sausages usually include red wine, juniper and herbs, which complement the flavour of the meat really well. They are great winter sausages and are especially delicious served with winter vegetables and red-wine gravy.

10 Toulouse This French classic is a meaty pork sausage flavoured with bacon, garlic, spices and red wine. It must be cooked before eating and is traditionally used in casseroles, especially cassoulet.

11 Weisswurst Cousin to Bratwurst but made richer by the addition of eggs and cream, this is a traditional white sausage from Germany.

12 Chicken These sausages are lower in fat than pork sausages, which makes them a healthier option and one that is growing in popularity. The basic recipe can be enhanced with additional flavourings (see p.39).

13 Cumberland This is a chunky, coarsely minced pork sausage that is highly seasoned with black pepper. It is available as a coil (see p.17) or as links. The coil variety is sometimes sold by length rather than weight. It is then either cooked whole or cut into pieces. Cook it as you would cook country pork sausages.

14 White pudding White pudding comes in many guises, with the ingredients varying according to where it is made. In Scotland it consists of suet, oatmeal, onion and spices and is known as 'mealy' pudding. The French version – boudin blanc – is made of pork, eggs and milk; it is forbidden to include any cereal element.

White puddings are usually pre-cooked and only need reheating before eating. Reheating usually means frying or grilling, as with black pudding (see opposite). White pudding is good with apples and wild mushrooms.

15 Beef Made with beef, herbs and spices, these are the preferred sausage in Scotland.

16 Boerewors A South African 'farmer's' sausage made from a mixture of beef and pork with coriander and red wine vinegar. It is delicious oven-baked or in stews and casseroles.

17 Oxford This is a regional sausage which dates back to medieval times. It is traditionally made from a blend of pork and veal with grated lemon zest and aromatic herbs.

18 Mild Italian A classic Italian fresh sausage made from pork and mildly spiced with garlic and fennel seed, this sausage is often referred to as 'sweet' Italian. The variation with red chilli is known as Hot Italian (see p.36). It is very similar to luganega (see below), but is made in links rather than in a coil. All Italian-style fresh sausage is known generally as salsiccia.

19 Merguez This sausage comes from the countries of the Maghreb – Tunisia, Algeria and Morocco – and is made to conform with Islamic dietary requirements. It is a red sausage made from lamb or sometimes beef and varies in size from mini to standard sausage size. Harissa (a hot chilli sauce) is often used to add a spicy flavour. Merguez is wonderful added to meat tagines and served with couscous.

20 Lamb Lamb sausages are more popular in Mediterranean countries than in northern Europe with the exception being Wales, where sheep are widely reared. The basic recipe is often enhanced with leeks, mint or other flavourings (see p.39).

Sausages to buy

1 Luganega A coiled, semi-cured, Italian sausage flavoured with garlic and spices that is especially popular in Lombardy. It is wonderful fried or grilled, oven-baked with lentils or crumbled into pasta dishes.

2 Nduja From Calabria in Italy, this coarse-grained, extremely highly spiced pork-paste sausage is like a spreadable salami. It is delicious added to pasta dishes or served with ripe cheese.

3 Black pudding ring Made from congealed blood mixed with cereal, this sausage comes in traditional rings or in small 'chubbs'. It is popular in Britain where it is traditionally served as part of a hearty English breakfast and in France where it is called boudin noir. It is particularly good accompanied by sweet apples.

4 Haggis This sausage made from sheep's offal, nuts and cereal is associated with Scotland, where it is traditionally served on Burns Night (25 January) with neeps (mashed turnips) and tatties (mashed potato). Bought haggis is pre-cooked so you only need to re-heat it until it is piping hot. You can either cook it in the oven or wrap it in foil and poach it in simmering water.

5 Cured chorizo This dry-cured chorizo is generally eaten raw, cut into thin slices. Use it as you would use salami or mortadella.

6 Kabanos This long, thin, lightly smoked dry pork Polish sausage is part of the kielbasa (which means sausage in Polish) family. It is often flavoured with caraway seeds. Use it in soups, jambalaya and simple stir-fries, or serve it with onion, cabbage and potatoes.

7 Tuscan salami This is one of Italy's best-loved salamis. Delicately flavoured with pork fat and black pepper, it is great in salads and sandwiches or as part of an antipasti selection.

8 Chipolatas These thin pork sausages are popular as cocktail sausages served on sticks as a nibble to accompany drinks. They are delicious rolled in a sticky mix of honey and mustard and oven-baked.

9 Mortadella A large, pink, pre-cooked sausage from Bologna made from finely ground pork attractively flecked with fat and stuffed in beef bladders. It sometimes contains pistachios. Its uses are the same as salami. The American Bologna sausage is similar but smooth.

10 Pepperoni One of the world's most popular Italian sausages, pepperoni is used for classic pizza toppings. It is a thin, spicy salami-like cured sausage made from beef and pork. It has a chewy texture and gets its distinctive kick from the hot chilli used in its making.

11 Hog's pudding This old-fashioned white pudding from south-west England is made with pork and copious amounts of cereal. It is great for breakfast or served with shellfish, especially scallops.

12 Wild boar This traditional pork sausage is made from the meat of wild boar that are left to roam freely, which gives the meat a gamey flavour. Apple is often added to the meat mixture. Once associated with Italy, wild boar sausages are now much more widely available. These versatile sausages are delicious, fried, grilled or braised.

13 Lyon sausage This air-dried French sausage is made from lean pork, often with a little beef, and is highly seasoned with garlic. It has a marbling of fat, similar to mortadella (see number 9, above), but much finer. Lyon sausage is one of the most expensive, highly prized dried sausages. It is great in salads.

14 Lap cheong This firm, air-dried Chinese pork sausage looks similar to Italian pepperoni, but that is where the similarity ends. Unlike pepperoni, lap cheong has a somewhat sweet flavour and it is usually poached before being fried or grilled. It is great in salad, soups and stir-fries.

15 Morcilla Traditional Spanish blood sausage containing onions, rice and spices, and fairly heavily seasoned with salt. Use it as you would any blood sausage. It is especially tasty sliced into a casserole.

16 Saveloy Not to be confused with the Swiss cervelat, saveloy is a pre-cooked sausage made of emulsified sausage mix. It is popular in the north of England where it is often deep-fried in a crispy batter.

17 Cotechino This mild, fatty, pork-based Italian sausage is sold either cooked or uncooked. Both must be simmered over a low heat before serving and both must be pierced before cooking to allow some of the fat to drain out. Cotechino is traditionally served with lentils on New Year's Day (see my recipe on page 175) as it is thought to bring good luck for the year ahead. Cotechino can also be used in bollito misto, a dish of mixed boiled meats from northern Italy.

Sausages to make

(see pages 20–41)

1 Loukanika
2 Lincolnshire
3 Faggots
4 Country pork
5 Cajun andouille
6 Chorizo picante
7 Bratwurst
8 Bockwurst
9 Venison
10 Toulouse
11 Weisswurst
12 Chicken
13 Cumberland coil
14 White pudding
15 Beef
16 Boerewors
17 Oxford
18 Mild Italian
19 Merguez
20 Lamb

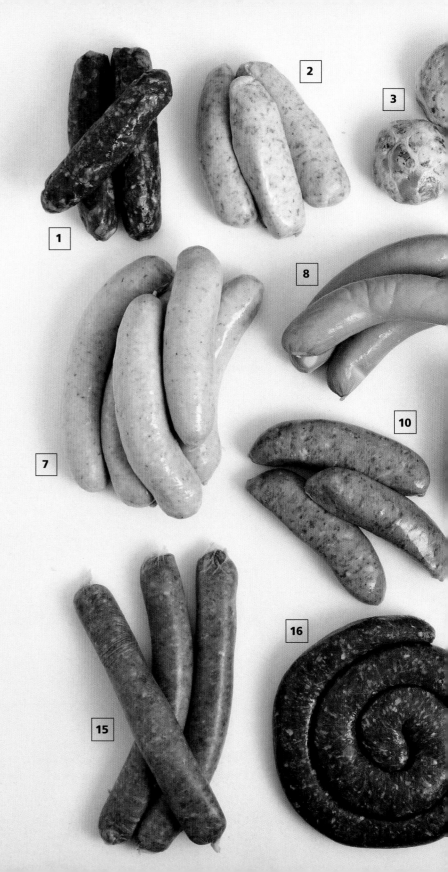

Sausages to buy

make your
own sausages

making fresh sausages

If you are used to eating factory-made sausages, eating your own home-made sausages will be a revelation. Making them is fun and easy too, as you will see from the following pages.

Apart from considerations of flavour, there are many advantages to making your own sausages. For a start you are in complete control of the quality of the ingredients, plus you have the opportunity to create your own personalised recipes, or adapt classic sausage recipes to suit your taste and budget.

If you prefer, you can buy ready-minced sausage meat from a butcher or have a butcher mince your own mixture of meats for you, but I think this defeats the object and takes away the fun and sense of achievement.

The basic steps for making your own sausages in casings from scratch are:

- mincing the meat or meats (see page 24)
- adding the herbs, spices and other flavourings
- stuffing the casings (see pages 25–6)
- tying the casings (see page 27)

THE INGREDIENTS
You can use any type of meat, either on its own or in combination with another, but pork is by far the most popular and easiest to handle.

Ideally your sausage meat mixture should consist of both lean and fatty meat. If you aim for a mix that's about 60 per cent lean meat to 40 per cent fatty meat, you won't go far wrong.

You can also use a small quantity – roughly 10 per cent – of filler such as breadcrumbs if you like. The most common herbs used to flavour sausages are marjoram, sage, parsley, thyme, oregano, rosemary, savory, basil and mint. Certain herbs are used in certain types of sausage – marjoram and sage, for example, are traditionally used in Cumberland sausages – but it is fun to ring the changes according to what is available seasonally.

Apart from the obvious salt and pepper, you can also flavour your sausages with any of a wide variety of ground spices. For example, choose from cumin, coriander, nutmeg, allspice, mace, ginger, chilli and paprika.

Some traditional sausage recipes also include a splash of wine or spirit, to add flavour but sometimes to act as a preservative too. Toulouse sausages are made with red wine while Greek loukanika sausages are made with white.

THE CASINGS AND WRAPPINGS
The casing that holds the sausage meat mixture together is vitally important. For best results, always choose casings made from animal (pig/hog or ox) intestines, rather than artificial casings made from cellulose and collagen. Sheep casings are best for cocktail-size sausages as they are smaller. You can buy casings from your butcher but you may need to order them in advance.

Natural casings are salted to preserve them, so soak them for at least four, and preferably 24 hours, before use. After soaking, it is also a good idea to run cold water through the casings to sluice out the insides.

As an alternative to stuffing your sausage meat into a casing, you might like to try your hand at making patty-style skinless sausages (see page 28), sausages wrapped in caul fat (crépine: see page 28), or sausages wrapped in clingfilm, which is removed before eating (see page 29).

mincing

Whichever type of mincer you use, make sure that the meat is well chilled and cut into dice before you start. Chilling ensures the meat flows freely through the mincer. It is a question of taste how finely you mince the meat. Personally, I think coarsely ground meat gives a nicer textured sausage.

1 Using a hand mincer A hand mincer is perfect if you are just starting out making sausages or if you only want to make a small batch of sausage meat. Clamp the mincer firmly to the table top or work surface, attach your preferred mincing plate and place a dish underneath. Feed a handful of chilled diced meat into the hopper and turn the handle. The minced meat will fall into the dish.

2 Using an electric mincer If you plan to make large quantities of home-made sausages, you can buy a dedicated electric meat mincer, but a mincer attachment that fits onto a standard kitchen mixing machine works just as well. As with the hand mincer, attach your preferred mincing plate and place a handful of chilled diced meat in the hopper. Turn the machine on at low speed, push the meat down the feed tube with the pusher provided, and catch the minced meat in a bowl.

3 Using a food processor Mincing sausage meat using a food processor is a little tricky as there is a risk of over-processing the meat and ending up with a paste. To avoid this, always use the pulse button and remember – less is more.

stuffing

In an ideal world, stuffing the casing with sausage meat is a two-person job, especially if you are a beginner sausage maker. One person pushes the meat through and the other holds the casing as it fills with meat. The principle is the same whichever stuffing method you choose.

using a piping bag

1 Fit a plain nozzle to a large piping bag and half-fill the bag with minced sausage meat. Do not over-fill the bag or the meat will be forced out of the top as you work. Slip one end of the casing over the nozzle so the casing forms accordion-like pleats.

2 One person holds the bag firmly at the top with one hand and places the other hand at the nozzle end, with the thumb over the end of the casing. The person holding the bag applies slow, even pressure to push the minced meat into the casing. The person holding the casing helps adjust the flow to ensure there are no pockets of air in the meat. To finish, follow the tying instructions on page 27.

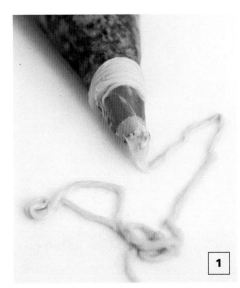

using the sausage stuffer attachment on an electric mixer

1 After you have minced the meat (see page 24, number 2), remove the mincing plate from the electric mincer and attach the sausage stuffing nozzle of your choice. Slip one end of the casing onto the nozzle so the casing forms accordion-like pleats.

2 Place the minced meat in the hopper and turn the machine on at low speed. One person pushes the meat down the feed tube with the pusher provided, while the other person holds the casing, adjusting the flow of the meat to ensure there are no pockets of air. To finish, follow the tying instructions on page 27.

using a sausage stuffing machine

1 Clamp the sausage stuffing machine to the table top or work surface and fill the barrel with the minced sausage meat.

2 Fit the filled barrel to the stuffing machine and lock it in place. Now attach the nozzle of your choice.

3 Slip one end of the sausage casing onto the nozzle so the casing forms accordion-like pleats over the nozzle.

4 One person should turn the handle gently to push the minced meat into the casing while the other holds the casing, adjusting the flow of the meat to ensure there are no pockets of air. For a more tightly packed sausage, hold the casing back slightly as the handle is turned. To finish, follow the tying instructions on the opposite page.

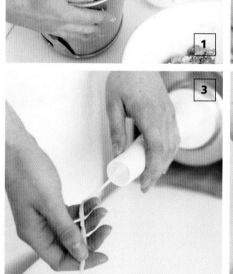

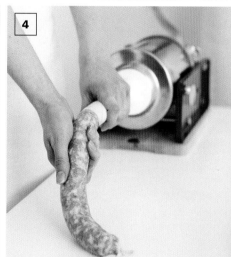

tying

1 When the casing is full, remove it from whichever filling attachment you have used and tie a knot in one end.

2 Decide on the length of sausage you want, pinch the sausage at that point and twist it clockwise several times. Then pinch at the end of the next sausage, this time twisting anti-clockwise. Repeat along the whole length of the stuffed casing.

3 If you prefer, you can tie the ends of each sausage with some fine kitchen string.

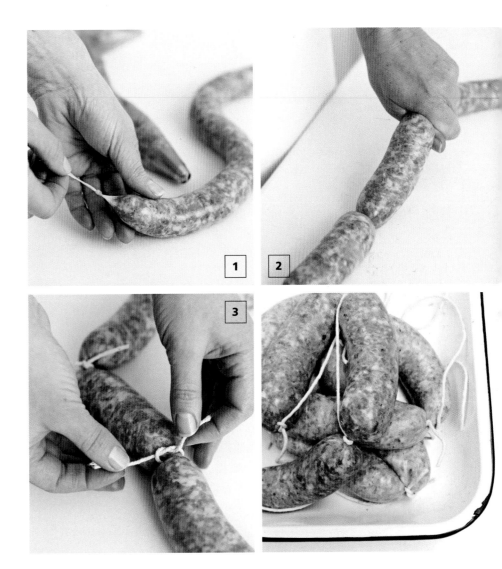

making skinless sausages

patties

1 Scoop up a handful of the prepared sausage mixture.

2 Using wetted hands, roll the mixture into a ball between your palms.

3 Pat the ball to flatten it or, if preferred, form it into a sausage shape.

wrapping in caul fat (crépine)

1 Soak the caul fat for 1–2 hours in cold water then remove and cut into 15–20cm (6–8in) squares.

2 Follow steps 1 and 2 above, then lay each ball on a square of caul fat and wrap the fat round to cover the meat completely.

wrapping in clingfilm

1 Place a line of prepared sausage meat on a piece of clingfilm.

2 Roll the meat into a sausage shape.

3 Cut the piece of clingfilm, leaving a 5cm (2in) margin all round the sausage shape. Tie the clingfilm into a knot at each end.

4 Steam for 15 minutes in a steamer or colander over a pan of boiling water. Allow to cool slightly before unwrapping then fry or grill for 10 minutes. Alternatively, poach in a poaching pan for 10 minutes before frying or grilling.

Country pork sausages YIELD 12 X 90G (3OZ) SAUSAGES

If, like me, you enjoy the taste of plump, well-made pork sausages, this recipe is just the job. These sausages are also commonly known as breakfast or link sausages. Ideally, try and make them using pork from a rare breed, but if you can't find that, then don't worry. Your sausages will taste fantastic anyway.

500g (1lb 2oz) lean neck or leg of pork, skinless and boneless

200g (7oz) boneless belly of pork, rind removed

250g (9oz) pork back fat

1 tsp finely chopped thyme leaves

½ tbsp finely chopped flat-leaf parsley

6 sage leaves, finely chopped

generous pinch of ground mace

1 tbsp sea salt

2 tsp freshly ground black pepper

2m (6½ft) pre-soaked hog casings (see p.22)

1 The day before, put the pork, belly of pork and back fat in the fridge and leave overnight.
2 The next day, cut into dice, pass through a coarse mincer (see p.24), then add the thyme, parsley, sage, mace and salt and pepper and mix well.
3 Fill the sausage casings with the mixture using your preferred method (see pp.25–6), form into links, then leave in the fridge until required.

VARIATIONS

PORK AND APPLE SAUSAGES (ALSO KNOWN AS SOMERSET SAUSAGES)

Add 100g (3½oz) of fresh white breadcrumbs and 2 peeled and finely chopped Bramley cooking apples to the basic mixture, then proceed according to the recipe above.

PORK AND CHILLI SAUSAGES

Replace the thyme in the recipe with ½ tsp of dried red chilli flakes.

PORK AND HERB SAUSAGES

Replace the thyme and flat-leaf parsley with the same amount of herbs of your choice, for example, rosemary, savory, sage and chives, then proceed according to the recipe above.

PORK AND LEEK SAUSAGES (ALSO KNOWN AS WELSH SAUSAGES)

Add 200g (7oz) of finely chopped leek and 100g (3½oz) of fresh white breadcrumbs to the basic mixture, then proceed according to the recipe above.

PORK AND STILTON SAUSAGES

Add 150g (5½oz) of crumbled Stilton to the basic mixture then proceed according to the recipe above.

PORK, TOMATO AND BASIL SAUSAGES

Replace the thyme and flat-leaf parsley with the same amount of freshly chopped basil leaves and add 150g (5½oz) of drained and finely chopped sunblush tomatoes. Proceed according to the recipe above.

LINCOLNSHIRE SAUSAGES

Replace the thyme and flat-leaf parsley with 10 leaves of finely chopped fresh sage, then proceed according to the recipe above. You can mince the meat more coarsely if you want a more authentic sausage.

Classic Cumberland sausages YIELD 15 X 90G (3OZ) SAUSAGES

These are classic mild pork sausages enhanced with fresh marjoram and sage, and with a kick of spicy black pepper. They're a great all-rounder. Try them as part of a great British fried breakfast or eat them grilled, in casseroles, or oven-baked as in toad-in-the-hole (see page 150). You can make this recipe into a traditional coiled spiral or into individual links, as you prefer.

450g (1lb) boneless shoulder of pork, diced

450g (1lb) boneless belly of pork, rind removed and diced

200g (7oz) pork back fat, diced

75g (2½oz) fresh white breadcrumbs

1 tbsp finely chopped marjoram leaves

2 tbsp finely chopped sage leaves

1 tsp freshly cracked black pepper

1 tbsp sea salt

generous pinch each of cayenne, ground mace and nutmeg

2m (6½ft) pre-soaked hog casings (see p.22)

1 The day before, mix together all the ingredients except the hog casings in a large bowl, cover with clingfilm and leave overnight in the fridge.

2 The next day, pass the mixture through a coarse mincer (see p.24).

3 Fill the sausage casings with the mixture using your preferred method (see pp.25–6). Form into links or leave as a coil. Leave in the fridge until required.

Toulouse sausages YIELD 15 X 90G (3OZ) SAUSAGES

A great French sausage with a long pedigree, the Toulouse sausage is made of pork, spices and red wine, highly flavoured with garlic. It's an all-round winner that's particularly good in casseroles and other oven-cooked dishes like my Simple sausage cassoulet on page 160.

1.25kg (2¾lb) boneless belly of pork, cut into large dice

400g (14oz) pork back fat, cut into large dice

200g (7oz) diced bacon

½ tsp caster sugar

¼ tsp ground mace

4 garlic cloves, crushed

100ml (3½fl oz) red wine

salt and freshly ground black pepper

2m (6½ft) pre-soaked hog casings (see p.22)

1 The day before, put the belly of pork, pork back fat and bacon in a large bowl. Add the sugar, mace, garlic and red wine, and season with salt and pepper to taste. Mix well, then cover with clingfilm and leave overnight in the fridge.

2 The next day, pass the mixture through a coarse mincer (see p.24).

3 Fill the sausage casings with the mixture using your preferred method (see pp.25–6), form into links, then leave in the fridge until required.

Chorizo picante sausages YIELD 20 X 90G (3OZ) SAUSAGES

Here's my recipe for fresh chorizo picante. The recipe is typically Spanish, as you'd expect. It's well seasoned with garlic and warmly spiced with the ever-popular pimentón, or smoked paprika. Once you've made your chorizos, enjoy them grilled or fried, or add them to eggs or stews.

1kg (2¼lb) boneless shoulder of pork, cut into large dice

1.5kg (3lb 3oz) belly of pork, cut into large dice

6 tsp smoked paprika (pimentón)

1 medium onion, finely chopped or grated

100ml (3½fl oz) white wine

3 garlic cloves, crushed

1–2 tsp cayenne pepper

½ tsp ground cumin

1 tsp ground fennel

salt and freshly ground black pepper

2m (6½ft) pre-soaked hog casings (see p.22)

1 Mix together all the ingredients except the hog casings in a large bowl, cover with clingfilm and leave in the fridge for 24 hours for the meats to fully absorb the liquids.

2 The next day, pass the mixture through a coarse mincer (see p.24).

3 Fill the sausage casings with the mixture using your preferred method (see pp.25–6), form into links, then leave in the fridge until required.

White pudding YIELD 12 X 90G (3OZ) SAUSAGES

White pudding is a popular British and French sausage. In Britain it is formed into large, thick sausages that are generally enclosed in casings of tripe skin. This is difficult to obtain, so use hog casings instead. The pudding may be cooked whole, though it is generally cut into slices and pan-fried.

150ml (¼ pint) full-fat milk

150ml (¼ pint) double cream

2 medium onions, finely chopped

120g scant (4½oz) oatmeal or fresh white breadcrumbs

500g (1lb 2oz) lean pork or leg

150g (5½oz) pork back fat

100g (3½oz) beef suet

1 free-range egg, beaten

1 tsp ground allspice

salt and freshly ground black pepper

2m (6½ft) pre-soaked hog casings (see p.22)

1 Put the milk and cream in a pan over a medium heat and bring to the boil, then pour the hot mixture over the onions in a bowl and leave for 15 minutes.

2 Strain the mixture over the oatmeal or breadcrumbs and leave to cool.

3 Meanwhile, finely mince the pork, pork back fat and suet (see p.24) into a bowl, then add the egg and the onion and oatmeal mixture. Season with allspice and salt and pepper to taste, and leave in the fridge for 2 hours to firm up.

4 Fill the sausage casings with the mixture using your preferred method (see pp.25–6), then form into links.

5 Bring a pan of water to 82°C (180°F), add the sausages and poach them at this temperature for 18 minutes. Remove with a slotted spoon to a plate and leave to cool. Leave in the fridge until required.

Cajun andouille sausages YIELD 12 X 90G (3OZ) SAUSAGES

Andouille is a French sausage, first brought to Louisiana by French colonists. The best-known andouille in the USA is Cajun andouille, which gets its unique flavour by being smoked very slowly over pecan-wood chips. My version is unsmoked but still has a great flavour, redolent of pungent spices and garlic.

500g (1lb 2oz) leg or neck of pork, skinless and boneless

250g (9oz) boneless belly of pork, rind removed

150g (5½oz) pork back fat

8 garlic cloves, crushed

1 onion, finely grated

2 tbsp cracked black pepper

1 tsp cayenne pepper

2 tsp finely chopped thyme leaves

½ tsp sweet paprika

100ml (3½fl oz) dry white wine

sea salt to taste

2m (6½ft) pre-soaked hog casings (see p.22)

1 The day before, put the pork, belly of pork and back fat in the fridge and leave overnight.

2 The next day, cut half the meat and fat into 1cm (½in) dice, pass the remaining meat and fat through a coarse mincer (see p.24), then mix with the diced meat and fat.

3 Add the garlic, onion, pepper, cayenne, thyme, paprika, wine and salt, and mix well.

4 Fill the sausage casings with the mixture using your preferred method (see pp.25–6), form into links, then refrigerate for 2–3 days to allow the flavours to develop.

Oxford sausages YIELD 15 X 90G (3OZ) SAUSAGES

This regional British sausage dates back to the eighteenth century, when it was fried as a patty instead of being made into links. Made with pork and veal, or sometimes lamb, these sausages are flavoured with lemon zest and herbs. I'm pleased to say they're now regaining their popularity.

400g (14oz) boneless shoulder of pork, cut into large dice

400g (14oz) cushion or flank of veal, cut into large dice

2 tbsp finely chopped sage leaves

1 tsp finely chopped thyme leaves

1 tsp finely chopped rosemary leaves

150g (5½oz) shredded suet

250g (9oz) fresh white breadcrumbs

grated zest of 1 lemon

1 tsp ground nutmeg

salt and freshly ground black pepper

2m (6½ft) pre-soaked hog casings (see p.22)

1 Place the pork and veal in a large bowl. Add the sage, thyme and rosemary, cover and leave for 2 hours at room temperature.

2 Pass the mixture through a coarse mincer (see p.24), then add the shredded suet, breadcrumbs, lemon zest, nutmeg, and salt and pepper to taste. Mix well.

3 Fill the sausage casings with the mixture using your preferred method (see pp.25–6), form into links, then leave in the fridge until required.

Old-fashioned faggots YIELD 12 X 75G (2½OZ) FAGGOTS

This type of meatball is traditionally made in Britain, especially in the north of England. Sadly, faggots have fallen from favour, but I think the time is right to propel them back to stardom.

200g (7oz) pig's liver, cleaned of all sinew and cut into small dice

500g (1lb 2oz) boneless belly of pork, cut into small dice

100g (3½oz) pig's heart, cleaned of all sinew and cut into small dice

1 medium onion, finely chopped

½ garlic clove, crushed

generous pinch each of mace and ground cinnamon

2 free-range eggs, beaten

150g (5½oz) fresh white breadcrumbs

1 tbsp finely chopped sage leaves

salt and freshly ground black pepper

400g (14oz) caul fat (crépine)

1 Pass half the liver and the pork through a coarse mincer (see p.24) into a bowl, then add the remaining liver and the heart, followed by the onion, garlic, mace, cinnamon and eggs. Mix well.

2 Add the breadcrumbs and sage, season with salt and pepper to taste, and mix again.

3 Shape the mixture into small balls about 5cm (2in) in diameter and wrap each in a piece of caul fat (see p.28).

4 Leave in the fridge until required, then cook as you would normal sausages.

Oxford sausages

Mild Italian pork sausages   YIELD 15 X 90G (3OZ) SAUSAGES

Sausage-making in Italy varies from region to region, with each region having its own favourite. Most Italian sausages are made from pork that is mildly seasoned with herbs and garlic and sometimes with fennel seeds. In some areas, they prefer a spicier sausage, which they achieve by adding some red chilli flakes. This basic recipe for what is often referred to as 'sweet' Italian sausage should suit all tastes.

2 tbsp fennel seeds

1kg (2¼lb) boneless shoulder of pork, cut into large dice

400g (14oz) pork back fat, cut into large dice

2 garlic cloves, crushed

2 tbsp coarsely chopped flat-leaf parsley or sweet basil

100ml (3½fl oz) iced water

pinch of caster sugar

pinch of ground nutmeg

salt and freshly ground black pepper

2m (6½ft) pre-soaked hog casings (see p.22)

1 Heat a dry frying pan over a medium heat. Add the fennel seeds and toast lightly for 30 seconds to release their aroma.

2 Pass the pork and back fat through a coarse mincer (see p.24) into a bowl, then add the fennel seeds, garlic, parsley or basil, water, sugar, nutmeg, and salt and pepper to taste. Mix well.

3 Fill the sausage casings with the mixture using your preferred method (see pp.25–6), form into links, then leave in the fridge until required.

VARIATIONS

HOT ITALIAN PORK SAUSAGES

Add ½ tsp of red chilli flakes and 1 tsp of finely chopped oregano leaves to the basic mixture, then proceed according to the recipe above.

SICILIAN SAUSAGES

Replace the flat-leaf parsley with 1 tbsp each of coarsely chopped basil and oregano leaves, and replace the water with the same volume of red wine. Proceed according to the recipe above.

Bratwurst YIELD 12 X 90G (3OZ) SAUSAGES

Germany is the home of the veal sausage, or Bratwurst. It is often made with emulsified meat, so when you make these sausages at home, use a food processor and you'll achieve a similar result.

200ml (7fl oz) full-fat milk

1 medium onion, finely chopped

125g (4½oz) fresh white breadcrumbs

400g (14oz) flank or topside of veal, with no visible fat

200g (7oz) lean pork

150g (5½oz) pork back fat

1 free-range egg, beaten

1 tsp ground mace

½ tsp ground ginger

1 tsp ground allspice

a little grated nutmeg

salt and freshly ground white pepper

2m (6½ft) pre-soaked hog casings (see p.22)

1 Put the milk in a pan over a medium heat and bring to the boil. Pour the hot mixture over the onion in a bowl and leave for 10 minutes, then strain the milk over the breadcrumbs and leave to cool.

2 Meanwhile, put the veal, pork and back fat into a food processor and blitz to a paste-like consistency. Remove to a bowl, then add the egg, soaked breadcrumbs, mace, ginger and allspice. Season with nutmeg, salt and pepper to taste, then place in the fridge for 2 hours to firm up.

3 Fill the sausage casings with the mixture using your preferred method (see pp.25–6), then form into links.

4 Bring a pan of water to 82°C (180°F), add the sausages and poach at this temperature for 18 minutes. Remove with a slotted spoon to a plate and leave to cool. Leave in the fridge until required.

VARIATION

WEISSWURST

Replace the milk with 200ml (7fl oz) of double cream, then proceed according to the recipe above. This gives a creamier, richer sausage.

Beef sausages YIELD 15 X 90G (3OZ) SAUSAGES

Beef sausages are a far meatier affair than pork sausages and in Scotland they're generally the sausage of choice. You can replace most of the pork sausages in the recipes in this book with beef sausages.

1kg (2¼lb) chuck or skirt of beef

500g (1lb 2oz) beef suet or pork fat

½ tsp ground mace

2 tsp coarsely chopped thyme leaves

4 sage leaves, chopped

50g (1¾oz) fresh white breadcrumbs

1 tbsp sea salt

2 tsp freshly ground black pepper

2m (6½ft) pre-soaked ox or hog casings (see p.22)

1 The day before, put the beef and the suet or fat in the fridge and leave overnight. The next day, cut into small dice and pass through a coarse mincer (see p.24), then add the mace, thyme, sage, breadcrumbs, and salt and pepper and mix together well.

2 Fill the sausage casings with the mixture using your preferred method (see pp.25–6), form into links, then leave in the fridge until required.

VARIATION

BEEF AND ALE SAUSAGES

Add 100ml (3½fl oz) of your favourite ale and 50g (1¾oz) of fresh white breadcrumbs to the basic mixture, then proceed according to the recipe above.

Merguez YIELD 15 X 90G (3OZ) SAUSAGES OR 30 MINI MERGUEZ

This is a spicy red sausage with attitude. Use it to add a kick to dishes such as couscous, tagines, stews and casseroles. Merguez can also be made with beef instead of lamb.

1.25kg (2¾lb) lean boneless lamb shoulder

1kg (2¼lb) fatty boneless lamb shoulder

400g (14oz) lamb fat, diced

4 large plump garlic cloves, crushed

1 tsp fennel seeds, lightly toasted and ground

1 tbsp good-quality harissa

1 tsp chilli powder

½ tsp sweet paprika

½ tsp ground coriander

¼ tsp ground cumin

salt and freshly ground black pepper

2m (6½ft) pre-soaked lamb or hog casings (see p.22)

1 The day before, mix together all the ingredients except the casings and the salt and pepper in a large bowl. Cover with clingfilm and leave overnight in the fridge to allow the flavours to develop.

2 The next day, pass the mixture through a coarse mincer (see p.24). Season with salt and pepper to taste.

3 Fill the sausage casings with the mixture using your preferred method (see pp.25–6), form into links, then leave in the fridge until required. If you use lamb casings, your sausages will be smaller in diameter.

During the summer months I, like many people, love cooking sausages on the barbecue. This method adds a delicious, smoky taste. Cook your sausages slowly on the edge of the barbecue where the heat is less intense to ensure that your sausages cook evenly. And, as already mentioned, only turn them once or twice during cooking.

Some people like to poach their sausages for five minutes in a little simmering water, then finish them off on the barbecue. This can take away some of the worry about getting a barbecued sausage cooked right through (I'm sure you've been presented with a barbecued sausage that's burnt on the outside and half-raw inside!), but it's not something I'd ever bother to do.

OVEN-BAKING

If I'm in a particularly lazy mood, I simply plonk my sausages in a roasting tin with two tablespoons of oil and throw them in a moderate oven (180°–190°C/350°–375°F/ Gas 4–5) for 20–25 minutes. This cooking method is simple, foolproof and mess-free, and it's ideal for preparing a large number of sausages in one go. There's something about the all-round heat of oven-baking that gives a terrific result. Some cooks like to pre-heat the oil in the tin before adding the sausages but I don't think it makes much difference.

It can be a flavour revelation to brush oven-baked sausages with an interesting glaze as they cook. You could try smearing them just with mustard or with a honey-and-mustard glaze, with sweet chilli sauce or simply with your favourite mix of fresh herbs.

Alternatively, you can try adding a little stock or a sauce to the sausages. Spoon this over from time to time while the sausages are baking to keep them wonderfully moist.

BRAISING AND CASSEROLING

Braising and casseroling are good ways of cooking most sausages. You first have to brown the sausages with a little oil in a casserole or pan, cover them with stock or a sauce, then cook them slowly, either on a low heat for braising or in a moderate oven. As the sausages cook, the flavour develops within the dish. The sausages can be either whole or cut into chunks or thick slices.

POACHING

Poaching sausages is the least popular cooking method in Great Britain although it is fairly common in other parts of Europe and in the USA.

Italian cotechino sausage (see page 15), for example, whether of the cooked or uncooked variety, needs poaching before it is ready to eat. Similarly, some Asian sausages, such as lap cheong (see page 15) need poaching.

Sometimes poaching is used before another cooking method. Most German-style sausages, such as Bratwurst (see page 14) and Bockwurst (see page 14) for example, are poached first then fried or grilled.

For poaching, you need to have the water barely simmering. Bring the water to the boil, then keep it at around 65°C (150°F) and poach for 8–10 minutes. You will need up to 20 minutes for larger sausages such as cotechino. If you poach the sausages at too high a temperature, the skins will burst.

If you are serving your sausages poached rather than frying or grilling them after poaching, keep them moist in the poaching water until you are ready to serve them.

breakfasts and
light meals

Bruschetta with nduja and burrata

Tuscan-style bruschettas are very versatile. You can add all manner of interesting toppings. This combination of spicy nduja sausage, juicy tomatoes and creamy burrata cheese is simply delicious. For a more substantial meal, serve with a salad of chicory and rocket and a simple oil-and-vinegar dressing.

4 tbsp good-quality olive oil

120g scant (4½oz) nduja sausage, skin removed

4 slices of rustic-style bread (such as ciabatta or Pugliese)

2 plum tomatoes, peeled and cut into 4 thick slices

½ garlic clove, peeled and bruised

125g (4½oz) fresh burrata or buffalo mozzarella cheese

1 Heat half the oil in a frying pan over a medium heat. Add the sausage and fry for 2–3 minutes until golden, breaking the sausage up with a wooden spoon as it cooks. Remove from the heat and cover with a lid to keep warm.

2 Meanwhile, heat a ribbed griddle over a high heat until hot and slightly smoking. Add the slices of bread and toast on both sides until lightly charred. Set aside.

3 Brush the slices of tomato with the remaining oil and rub with the bruised garlic.

4 Arrange the tomato slices on top of the toasted bread and spoon over the cooked njuda sausage with its pan juices.

5 Top each bruschetta with a wedge of burrata cheese and serve immediately.

Baked chorizo and Emmenthal croissants

When you're looking for something that little bit different for breakfast, here's the answer – a hot, savoury croissant packed with spicy sausage and oozing Emmenthal cheese. You can make these croissants a little in advance, but not too early as they'll go soggy.

250–300g (9–10oz) chorizo picante (see p.32), skin removed

1 tbsp olive oil

½ small onion, finely chopped

¼ tsp chopped thyme leaves

300ml (½ pint) full-fat milk

25g (scant 1oz) unsalted butter

25g (scant 1oz) plain flour

100g (3½oz) Emmenthal cheese, coarsely grated

8 fresh good-quality croissants

1 Preheat the oven to 200°C (400°F/Gas 6).

2 Cut the chorizo into thin slices.

3 Heat the oil in a frying pan over a medium heat. Add the sliced sausages, onion and thyme and fry for 5 minutes, stirring occasionally. Remove with a slotted spoon and set aside.

4 Meanwhile, warm the milk in a pan over a low heat. Keep warm.

5 Melt the butter in another pan over a low heat. Add the flour and stir with a wooden spoon to form a smooth light-brown paste or roux. Cook for 1 minute.

6 Add the hot milk and mix well to form a thick smooth sauce. Cook for 10 minutes, stirring frequently to ensure the sauce does not burn.

7 Add the cheese and mix well. Continue cooking for 10 minutes, stirring frequently. Remove from the heat.

8 Slice horizontally through the croissants, leaving a hinge. Mix the sausage with the sauce and use to carefully fill each croissant.

9 Place the croissants on a baking sheet and bake in the preheated oven for 5 minutes, or until each croissant and its filling are hot. Serve warm.

Breakfast quesadillas

When I worked in America, I seemed to eat quesadillas every day. I just love them! This a great breakfast or brunch recipe. The quesadillas can be prepared ahead, kept in the fridge, and finished when needed.

300g (11oz) new potatoes

2 tbsp olive oil

6 fresh country pork sausages (see p.30), thinly sliced

8 flour tortillas, each approx 20cm (8in) in diameter

4 spring onions, trimmed and thinly sliced

½ small red chilli, deseeded and finely chopped

2 hard-boiled free-range eggs, coarsely chopped

300g (11oz) Cheddar cheese, coarsely grated

salt and freshly ground black pepper

1 Peel the potatoes and cut into 1cm (½in) dice. Put in a pan of lightly salted water, bring to the boil, reduce the heat and cook for 15 minutes, or until tender. Drain and set aside.

2 Heat the oil in a non-stick frying pan over a medium heat. Add the sausage slices and cook for 10 minutes, stirring occasionally until cooked and golden. Remove with a slotted spoon and set aside.

3 Add the cooked potatoes to the pan and fry, stirring regularly, until golden. Season with salt and pepper to taste. Transfer to a bowl and leave until cool.

4 Lay 4 of the tortillas out on a flat surface. Sprinkle each evenly with all the remaining ingredients. Top with the remaining 4 tortillas and press down lightly with a plate. Chill in the fridge for 30 minutes.

5 Heat a non-stick frying pan over a medium heat. Add the quesadillas and cook for 2–3 minutes on each side, or until they are golden and the cheese has melted. Turn out, cut each quesadilla into 4 wedges and serve immediately.

Muffaletta

I got the idea for this Sicilian-style sandwich from a dish I ate in a New York deli but it really originates in New Orleans. There are many variations, some of which include olives, but I prefer it without.

4 large soft baps or any soft or crusty roll

25g (scant 1oz) unsalted butter

12 small garlic cloves, crushed

1 tsp Dijon mustard

2 tbsp finely chopped basil leaves

4 slices of mortadella sausage

12 slices of Tuscan salami

2 ready-to-serve roasted red peppers, drained, deseeded and finely shredded

4 small ripe plum tomatoes, thinly sliced

1 buffalo mozzarella, thinly sliced

100g (3½oz) provolone cheese, thinly sliced

1 Preheat the oven to 180°C (350°F/Gas 4).

2 Slice the baps in half and set aside.

3 Put the butter, garlic, mustard and basil in a bowl and mix well.

4 Spread the butter and herb mixture on 4 of the bap halves.

5 Lay all the remaining ingredients on top in alternating slices, pressing down lightly as you go. Top with the remaining bap halves.

6 Wrap each bap in a piece of greaseproof paper, then place in the preheated oven for 5–6 minutes, or until the baps are heated through and the cheese is beginning to melt. Remove from the oven and leave to cool slightly before serving.

Quesadillas

Spicy baked eggs

Eggs are one of my favourite ingredients, especially in breakfast or brunch dishes. I love them cooked all ways. In this terrific dish, they're baked with chorizo and a spicy tomato-based sauce. Serve with lots of country-style rustic bread to dip into the soft-cooked eggs.

½ tsp saffron strands or powdered saffron

250ml (8fl oz) hot chicken stock

2 tbsp olive oil

100g (3½oz) chorizo picante (see p.32) or loukanika, skin removed and coarsely chopped

1 medium onion, finely chopped

2 garlic cloves, crushed

1 small red chilli, deseeded and finely chopped

1 tsp smoked paprika

1 tbsp white wine vinegar

2 x 400g (14oz) tins peeled plum tomatoes

75g (2½oz) peas, fresh or frozen

2 spring onions, trimmed and finely chopped

8 free-range eggs

salt and freshly ground black pepper

crusty bread, to serve

1 Preheat the oven to 200°C (400°F/Gas 6).

2 Place the saffron in the hot chicken stock and leave to infuse for 5 minutes. Meanwhile, heat 1 tbsp of the oil over a medium heat in a frying pan. Add the chopped chorizo and fry for 1 minute until it is golden and the fat has been released. Remove with a slotted spoon and set aside.

3 Add the onion, garlic and chilli to the pan and cook over a medium heat until softened. Add the smoked paprika and wine vinegar, and cook for 30 seconds more. Add the saffron-infused chicken stock and the tomatoes and their juice, and bring to the boil.

4 Reduce the heat to low, add the peas and spring onions, and return the fried chorizo to the pan. Simmer for 10 minutes.

5 Divide the chorizo mixture between four 10cm (4in) ovenproof dishes. Crack 2 eggs on top of each, season with salt and pepper to taste, then place in the preheated oven for 5–6 minutes, or until the eggs are set. Bake for longer if you prefer your eggs more cooked.

6 Drizzle over the remaining oil and serve immediately with crusty bread.

Hog's pudding with scallops
and apple butter

Hog's pudding is a speciality pork sausage from the West Country of England. It's made from pork and offal bound with oatmeal and a little suet, in the style of a classic white pudding. People sometimes describe it as 'Devonshire haggis', though I fail to see the similarity. This recipe makes a delicious gourmet breakfast or light meal.

400g (14oz) floury potatoes
(such as Maris Piper or King Edward)

200g (7oz) cooked green cabbage,
finely shredded

20g (¾oz) unsalted butter

15g (½oz) plain flour

4 tbsp olive oil

2 hog's puddings, skin removed and
cut into 10cm (4in) slices

8 rashers streaky bacon

8 large scallops, removed from their
shells (including roe if liked)

salt, white pepper and nutmeg

FOR THE APPLE BUTTER

1 Granny Smith apple

10g (¼oz) unsalted butter

1 tbsp caster sugar

1 tbsp rice wine vinegar

1 Peel the potatoes and cut into large chunks. Put in a pan of lightly salted water, bring to the boil, reduce the heat and cook for 12–15 minutes, or until tender. Drain well then return to the pan, stirring over a low heat for a minute or two until dry. Mash until smooth.

2 Add the cabbage and 15g (½oz) of the butter. Mix well, season with salt, pepper and nutmeg, cook for 2–3 minutes, remove from the heat and leave to cool.

3 When cool, shape into 8 equal-sized potato cakes, dust liberally with the flour, remove excess flour, then chill in the fridge for 1 hour.

4 Make the apple butter. Peel and core the apple and cut into small dice.

5 Heat the butter in a pan over a low heat. When the butter has melted, add the apple and fry, stirring, for 2–3 minutes. Add the sugar and cook for 5 minutes more until caramelised and golden.

6 Add the rice wine vinegar and 3 tbsp of water. Cook for 1 minute more, then transfer to a blender and process to a thick purée. Return the purée to the pan and cover with a lid to keep warm.

7 When nearly ready to serve, heat half the oil in a large frying pan over a medium heat. Add the chilled potato cakes and fry for 2–3 minutes on each side until golden and crisp.

8 In another frying pan, heat the remaining butter and oil over a medium heat. When the fat is hot, add the sliced hog's pudding, bacon and scallops, and cook for 1–2 minutes on each side. Remove from the pan and season lightly with salt and pepper.

9 To serve, place 2 fried potato cakes on each of the 4 plates with some slices of fried hog's pudding alongside. Pour the pan juices over, dividing them between the plates, then top each potato cake with a spoonful of apple purée followed by a fried scallop and 2 rashers of bacon. Serve immediately.

The best sausage sarnie

Sausage sandwiches – known colloquially as sarnies or butties – have always been a favourite of mine at breakfast time and they're now becoming somewhat trendy. To make the perfect sausage sandwich, you need a good, thickly cut bloomer-style loaf, some tender fried onions, and a decent sausage – all finished with a side of tomato ketchup or brown sauce. Just writing this recipe makes me drool!

2 tbsp olive oil

8 Cumberland sausages (see p.31)

1 large onion, thinly sliced

8 thick slices of crusty farmhouse bloomer loaf

unsalted butter, for spreading

1 tbsp Dijon or prepared English mustard

salt and freshly ground black pepper

tomato ketchup or brown sauce, to serve

1 Heat the oil in a large frying pan over a medium heat. Add the sausages and cook for 18–20 minutes, stirring occasionally until golden and cooked through. Remove with a slotted spoon to a plate and cover with tinfoil to keep warm.

2 Add the onion to the pan and cook slowly for 10–12 minutes, stirring occasionally until golden and caramelised. Season with salt and pepper to taste.

3 Meanwhile, lightly butter the bread and generously smear 4 of the buttered slices with the mustard.

4 Top with the caramelised onions, cut the sausages in half and place 4 sausage halves on each of the 4 slices. Cover each with the remaining slices of bread. Press down gently to compact the sandwich.

5 To serve, cut each sandwich in half, place on a plate and serve with your favourite sauce.

Mint mustard sausage rolls

Sausage rolls are a real classic that can be eaten as a tasty snack, or at drinks parties or as part of a buffet. They're traditionally made with pork, but these are made with lamb. If you'd like to serve them as a nibble with drinks, you can make them smaller than suggested here. This recipe is a little more upscale!

450g (1lb) lamb and mint sausages (see p.39), skin removed

1 tbsp mint sauce

2 tbsp finely chopped mint leaves

½ medium onion, finely chopped

1 tsp prepared English mustard

200g (7oz) ready-rolled puff pastry

plain flour, for dusting

1 free-range egg, lightly beaten

salt and freshly ground black pepper

1 Preheat the oven to 190°C (375°F/Gas 5). Line a baking sheet with baking parchment.

2 In a bowl, combine the sausage meat, mint sauce, chopped mint, onion and mustard. Season with salt and pepper to taste and set aside.

3 Roll the pastry out on a lightly floured board to a thickness of about 5mm (¼in). Trim to a rectangle of 28 x 20cm (11 x 8in) then cut the rectangle in half lengthways.

4 Divide the sausage mixture into 2 and spread it the length of each pastry strip, leaving a 1cm (½in) border all round.

5 Roll each pastry strip tightly around the sausage mixture, brush the ends with some of the beaten egg and fold over to secure. Cut each roll into 4 equal pieces and place on the lined baking sheet.

6 Brush each sausage roll liberally with the remaining beaten egg, place in the oven and bake for 25–30 minutes, until the pastry is risen and golden and the meat is cooked through. Allow to cool slightly before serving.

soups

Clam and chorizo broth

The delicate briny flavour of clams works beautifully with the rich sausages and the saffron-infused broth. I always serve this soup with garlic bread with freshly chopped thyme added to the garlic butter.

2 tbsp olive oil

2 garlic cloves, crushed

1 medium onion, finely chopped

1 tsp smoked paprika

50g (1¾oz) chorizo picante (see p.32), skin removed and thinly sliced

50ml (scant 2fl oz) dry white wine

15ml (½fl oz) Pernod (optional)

a good pinch of saffron strands or ½ tsp powdered saffron

4 plum tomatoes, cut into 1cm (½in) dice

750ml (1¼ pints) fish or chicken stock

48 baby Venus clams

2 tbsp coarsely chopped flat-leaf parsley

1 Heat the oil in a pan over a medium heat. Add the garlic, chopped onion and paprika, and cook, stirring occasionally for 5 minutes, or until softened.

2 Add the sliced chorizo and cook for 2 minutes more.

3 Add the white wine and Pernod, if using, then add the saffron, tomatoes and stock. Bring to the boil, then reduce the heat and simmer for 5 minutes.

4 Add the clams, cover with a tight-fitting lid, and cook for 2 minutes, or until the clams open.

5 Discard any clams that do not open, then transfer to 4 soup bowls, sprinkle with the parsley and serve immediately.

Fennel and leek soup with sausage 'soldiers'

This is a delicious rustic soup whose taste and texture are both bound to please.

30g (1oz) unsalted butter

50g (1¾oz) streaky bacon, cut into small dice

1 head of fennel, trimmed and chopped

1 leek, cleaned, trimmed and sliced

½ tsp fennel seeds

1 litre (1¾ pints) chicken stock

100ml (3½fl oz) double cream

2 tbsp olive oil

salt and freshly ground black pepper

FOR THE SAUSAGE 'SOLDIERS'

2 tbsp olive oil

2–3 Oxford sausages (see p.34)

4 slices of thick white bread, crusts removed

30g (1oz) Cheddar cheese, coarsely grated

1 For the soup, heat the butter in a pan over a medium heat. When the butter is hot, add the bacon and fry for 5 minutes, turning occasionally until softened.

2 Add the fennel, leek and fennel seeds, cover and cook over a low heat for 8–10 minutes more.

3 Add the stock, bring to the boil, reduce the heat and simmer for 20 minutes.

4 Transfer to a blender and blitz until smooth. Return the soup to the pan, add the cream and season to taste.

5 To make the sausage 'soldiers', heat the oil in a frying pan over a medium heat. Add the sausages and fry, turning occasionally for 15–20 minutes, until golden and cooked through. Remove with a slotted spoon and cut into 5cm (2in) thick slices.

6 Cover 2 slices of the bread with the sausage, scatter over the cheese, then top with remaining slices of bread. Press down lightly to seal.

7 In a frying pan, heat the oil over a medium heat and fry the sausage sandwiches until golden and crispy on both sides.

8 Cut the sandwiches into 2.5cm (1in) thick slices to form 'soldiers'. Serve immediately with the soup.

Fennel and leek soup with sausage 'soldiers'

Sardinian fregola soup

This is a hearty soup from the Mediterranean. Fregola is a Sardinian pasta with a light smoky yet nutty flavour. It's like couscous in shape and size, but is firmer in texture. If you can't easily find it, you can use any small pasta shape instead. Ditalini are a good substitute.

4 tbsp olive oil

2 garlic cloves, crushed

1 medium onion, finely chopped

500g (1lb 2oz) pancetta, cut into small dice

300g (11oz) luganega sausages, skin removed

2 carrots, peeled and cut into small dice

½ small butternut squash, peeled, deseeded and cut into small dice

400g (14oz) tin cannellini beans, drained and rinsed

200g (7oz) tin peeled and chopped plum tomatoes

1 litre (1¾ pints) chicken or vegetable stock

300g (11oz) fregola pasta, or other small pasta

1 tsp finely chopped oregano

½ tsp finely chopped thyme leaves

½ tsp finely chopped rosemary leaves

salt and freshly ground black pepper

1 Heat half the oil in a pan over a medium heat. Add the garlic, onion and pancetta and cook over a medium heat for 2–3 minutes, stirring occasionally until they start to brown.

2 Add the sausages and fry for 4–5 minutes, breaking them up with a fork as they cook.

3 Add the carrots and squash, cover, reduce the heat and sweat for 4–5 minutes, or until soft.

4 Add the beans, tomatoes and stock. Increase the heat, bring to the boil, then stir in the fregola pasta. Reduce the heat and simmer for 10 minutes, or until the fregola is al dente.

5 Heat the remaining oil in a small pan over a gentle heat. Add the oregano, thyme and rosemary, and warm together for a few minutes.

6 Add the infused herb oil to the soup, season with salt and pepper to taste and serve immediately.

Italian sausage, egg
and Parmesan soup

If you want an extremely simple, satisfyingly flavourful soup, then this is it. The egg and Parmesan add a wonderful richness.

3 tbsp olive oil, plus extra to serve

1 medium onion, coarsely chopped

4 mild Italian sausages (see p.36), cut into 1cm (½in) dice

200g (7oz) tin peeled and chopped plum tomatoes

1 tbsp tomato purée

1 large potato

2 courgettes, cut into 1cm (½in) dice

1 stick celery, cut into 1cm (½in) dice

800ml (scant 1½ pints) chicken stock

12 basil leaves, coarsely chopped

2 tbsp coarsely chopped flat-leaf parsley

2 large free-range eggs

50g (1¾oz) Parmesan, finely grated

salt and freshly ground black pepper

1 Heat the oil in a heavy-based pan. Add the chopped onion and cook over a medium heat for 5 minutes, stirring occasionally until it begins to soften.

2 Add the sausages and fry for 5 minutes, stirring occasionally until browned all over.

3 Add the tomatoes and tomato purée, and cook for 5 minutes more.

4 Peel the potato and cut into 1cm (½in) dice.

5 Add the potato, courgettes and celery to the pan, cover, reduce the heat and sweat for 5 minutes, or until the vegetables have softened.

6 Uncover, pour over the stock and add 1 tsp salt and a little black pepper. Add the basil and parsley, increase the heat and bring to the boil.

7 Reduce the heat and simmer for 30 minutes, uncovered, until the vegetables are tender. Remove from the heat.

8 Beat the eggs and half the Parmesan together in a bowl, then pour into the soup in a thin stream, stirring constantly.

9 Divide the soup between 4 serving bowls, drizzle over a little olive oil, sprinkle over the remaining Parmesan and serve immediately.

Caldo verde is a staple soup of Portugal. It's simple to make and extremely heart-warming. My version includes podded broad beans together with Portuguese linguiça sausage. If you can't get this sausage, chorizo picante is a good alternative. Linguiça sausages are made with onions, garlic and paprika, which add a mildly spicy flavour. Serve with loads of chunky rustic bread.

My caldo verde

4 tbsp olive oil, plus extra to serve

1 large onion, coarsely chopped

2 garlic cloves, crushed

500g (1lb 2oz) waxy potatoes

1 litre (1¾ pints) vegetable stock or water

300g (11oz) kale or cabbage, finely shredded

150g (5½oz) broad beans, podded

150g (5½oz) linguiça sausages, thinly sliced

pinch of paprika

salt and freshly ground black pepper

1 Heat 3 tbsp of the oil in a heavy-based pan over a medium heat. Add the onion and garlic and cook for 5 minutes, stirring occasionally until they soften.

2 Peel and thinly slice the potatoes, then add to the pan together with the stock or water. Bring to the boil, reduce the heat and simmer for 25–30 minutes, or until the potatoes are soft.

3 Mash the potatoes into the soup to produce a coarse purée. Add the shredded kale or cabbage and the broad beans, reduce the heat and simmer for 5 minutes.

4 Heat the remaining oil in a frying pan, then add the sausage slices, sprinkle over a little paprika, and sauté for 2–3 minutes, stirring occasionally until golden and cooked through.

5 Season the soup to taste, then add the sautéed sausage. Divide the soup between 4 bowls, drizzle over a little olive oil and serve immediately.

Smoked corn and sausage chowder

You really need fresh corn on the cob for this recipe. The grilled corn and smoked sausage together impart a terrific smoky flavour to the soup.

4 corn on the cobs, husks removed

1 litre (1¾ pints) vegetable or chicken stock

50g (1¾oz) unsalted butter

1 medium onion, finely chopped

1 garlic clove, crushed

½ tsp ground cumin

4 corn tortillas, roughly chopped

250g (9oz) waxy potatoes

½ red pepper, deseeded and cut into small dice

½ green pepper, deseeded and cut into small dice

200g (7oz) Polish smoked kielbasa sausage, thinly sliced

150ml (¼ pint) double cream

pinch of sweet paprika

salt and freshly ground black pepper

1 Heat a ribbed griddle over a high heat until hot and slightly smoking. Add the corn cobs and grill for 10–15 minutes, turning occasionally until lightly charred but not burnt.

2 Remove and cool slightly, then scrape the kernels into a bowl with a knife. Set aside.

3 Chop the rest of the cobs into small pieces, place in a pan and cover with the stock. Bring to the boil, reduce the heat and simmer for 30 minutes, then strain, discarding the cobs and setting aside the stock.

4 Heat half the butter in another pan, add the onion, garlic, cumin and chopped tortillas, and cook over a low heat for 5 minutes, or until softened. Add the reserved corn kernels and stock, and simmer for 30 minutes, then transfer to a blender and blitz to a smooth liquid.

5 Meanwhile, peel the potatoes and cut into small dice.

6 Heat the remaining butter in another pan and cook the peppers, potatoes and sausage over a low heat for 10 minutes, stirring occasionally until the vegetables have softened.

7 Pour over the corn broth, add the cream and season with salt and pepper to taste and a little paprika. Transfer to serving bowls and serve immediately.

Merguez and black bean soup

This slightly spicy, heart-warming soup is ideal for a cold winter's day. If you like, you can substitute chickpeas for the black beans. They're equally delicious.

2 tbsp olive oil

1 large onion, coarsely chopped

1 large head of fennel, trimmed and coarsely chopped

3 garlic cloves, crushed

1 tsp smoked paprika

½ tsp ground cumin

375g (13oz) turtle beans, soaked overnight in cold water and drained

1 litre (1¾ pints) chicken stock

grated zest and juice of ½ lemon

150g (5½oz) merguez sausages (see p.38), thinly sliced

salt and freshly ground black pepper

sour cream, to serve (optional)

torn leaves of flat-leaf parsley, to garnish

1 Heat the oil in a heavy-based pan over a medium heat. Add the onion, fennel and garlic and cook for 2–3 minutes, stirring occasionally until softened.

2 Add the smoked paprika and cumin, and cook for 1 minute more, then add the beans and stock, and bring to the boil.

3 Reduce the heat and simmer for 1½–2 hours, or until the beans are tender, then transfer to a food processor and blitz until smooth. Season to taste with salt, pepper and lemon zest and juice. Return to the pan and keep warm.

4 Heat a frying pan over a medium heat. When the pan is hot, add the slices of merguez and sauté for 4–5 minutes, stirring occasionally until the sausage is golden and cooked through.

5 Serve the soup topped with the slices of sausage and with a spoonful of sour cream, if using. Garnish with torn flat-leaf parsley.

Kabanos and prawn gumbo

Gumbo is a hearty, spicy soup or main course from the American Deep South. There are many different recipes but all include some sort of spicy sausage. I like to allow the flavours of the sausage and prawns to speak for themselves. This gumbo can be fairly hot, so cut down on the Tabasco and cayenne if you prefer a milder taste. Kabanos is a long, dry, Polish pork sausage with a smoky flavour.

2 tbsp vegetable oil

1 medium onion, coarsely chopped

1 garlic clove, crushed

1 medium green pepper, deseeded and cut into 1cm (½in) dice

1 tbsp plain flour

800ml (scant 1½ pints) chicken stock

100g (3½oz) kabanos sausage, thinly sliced

125g (4½oz) okra, trimmed

½ tbsp finely chopped thyme leaves

1 bay leaf

pinch of salt

Tabasco sauce, to taste

pinch of cayenne pepper

200g (7oz) raw peeled tiger prawns, deveined and halved

2 spring onions, green part only, coarsely chopped

crusty bread or steamed rice, to serve

1 Heat the oil in a heavy-based pan over a medium heat. Add the chopped onion, garlic and pepper, and cook, stirring occasionally for 5 minutes, until softened.

2 Reduce the heat, add the flour and cook, stirring with a wooden spoon for 1 minute, until a smooth light-brown paste or roux forms.

3 Add the stock, a little at a time, stirring after each addition. Increase the heat and bring to the boil. Reduce the heat to a simmer, then stir until smooth.

4 Add the sausage, okra, thyme, bay leaf, a pinch of salt, the Tabasco and the cayenne pepper. Simmer over a low heat for 15 minutes.

5 Stir in the prawns and spring onions. Cook for 2–3 minutes more, then adjust the seasoning if required.

6 Remove the bay leaf and discard. Transfer to 4 soup bowls and serve immediately either with crusty bread or over steamed rice.

salads

Asian-inspired sausage salad

For this salad I prefer to use regular pork sausages rather than Asian ones. I think it keeps the flavours fresher and the dish lighter in texture. If you prefer to follow tradition, use lap cheong Chinese sausage. In Thailand they often serve this type of salad spooned over hot rice.

6 country pork sausages (see p.30)

½ cucumber, peeled and thinly sliced

2 Thai shallots or small red onions, thinly sliced

4 spring onions, trimmed and shredded diagonally

2 bird's eye chillies, very thinly sliced

1 tbsp Thai fish sauce (nam pla)

1 tbsp rice wine vinegar

2 tbsp palm sugar or soft brown sugar

juice of 2 limes

1 tsp light soy sauce

2 garlic cloves, very thinly sliced

4 plum tomatoes, halved, deseeded and cut into strips

Thai basil leaves, to garnish

coriander leaves, to garnish

1 Place the sausages in a pan of cold water and bring to the boil. Reduce the heat, then poach, uncovered, for 10 minutes. Remove with a slotted spoon and leave to cool.
2 Meanwhile, mix the remaining ingredients in a bowl, except the Thai basil and coriander. Toss well together to amalgamate the flavours.
3 Cut the cooled sausage into thin slices and add to the bowl. Toss again.
4 Transfer to 4 serving plates, sprinkle over the Thai basil and coriander and serve immediately.

Chorizo, beetroot and
bean salad with whipped feta

This makes a refreshing summer-inspired salad. Be sure to use good-quality feta cheese.

450g (1lb) small raw beetroot

275g (9½oz) broad beans, podded

2 tbsp coarsely chopped flat-leaf parsley

150g (5½oz) feta cheese

100ml (3½fl oz) sour cream

1 tbsp finely chopped mint leaves

250g (9oz) cured chorizo or Lyon sausage, thinly sliced

2 shallots, thinly sliced, to serve

salt and freshly ground black pepper

FOR THE DRESSING

2 tbsp sherry vinegar or red wine vinegar

4 tbsp olive oil

1 tbsp honey

1 tsp Dijon mustard

salt and freshly ground black pepper

1 Place the beetroot in a pan of cold water and bring to the boil. Reduce the heat, then simmer, uncovered, for 30 minutes, or until tender. Drain, leave to cool slightly and peel while still warm. Set aside.

2 Meanwhile, add the broad beans to a small pan of boiling salted water and cook for 2 minutes. Drain the beans and refresh in a colander under cold running water. Dry thoroughly in a clean tea towel and set aside.

3 For the dressing, whisk all the ingredients together in a bowl and season to taste.

4 Cut the beetroot into wedges and place in a bowl. Pour over the dressing, add the parsley and season to taste. Leave to marinate while you prepare the feta.

5 To prepare the feta, place in a bowl, break up with a wooden spoon until smooth, add the sour cream and mint, and mix well. Alternatively, process in a blender.

6 Add the beans to the beetroot and toss well together.

7 Divide the sliced chorizo between 4 serving plates in overlapping circles. Top with the bean and beetroot mixture and add a generous spoonful of whipped feta in the centre of each. Scatter the shallots around the salad and serve.

Salami, Emmenthal and cornichon salad

This simple salad is one I enjoy preparing any time. It's a great way to use up small leftovers of salami and Emmenthal cheese. It's delicious served with crusty bread.

2 Little Gem lettuces, leaves separated and torn into small pieces

1 Treviso or radicchio lettuce, leaves separated and torn into small pieces

1 Granny Smith apple, halved, cored and thinly sliced

75g (2½oz) walnut halves, lightly toasted

75g (2½oz) Emmenthal cheese, sliced then cut into matchsticks

50g (1¾oz) baby gherkins (cornichons), thinly sliced

200g (7oz) Tuscan salami sausage, skin removed and thinly sliced

FOR THE DRESSING

1 tsp Dijon mustard

1 tbsp white wine vinegar

1 tbsp crème fraîche

50ml (scant 2fl oz) good-quality mayonnaise

4 tbsp olive oil

salt and freshly ground black pepper

1 Place the pieces of lettuce in a bowl. Add the apple and walnuts and set aside.

2 Mix all the dressing ingredients together in a separate bowl. Season with salt and pepper to taste.

3 Lightly toss the salad with the dressing. Divide between 4 serving plates. Scatter over the cheese and gherkins. Lay the slices of salami on top.

Grilled squid, chorizo
and green olive salad with za'atar

400g (14oz) medium squid

1 tbsp olive oil

200g (7oz) chorizo picante (see p.32), skin removed and thinly sliced

12 cherry tomatoes, cut in half

25g (scant 1oz) rocket leaves

25g (scant 1oz) flat-leaf parsley

12 pitted plump green olives

salt and freshly ground black pepper

FOR THE DRESSING

juice of ¼ lemon

1 tbsp sherry vinegar

½ garlic clove, crushed

1 small red chilli, deseeded and finely chopped

4 tbsp olive oil

¼ tsp fennel seeds (optional)

salt and freshly ground black pepper

FOR THE ZA'ATAR

1 tsp sumac

1 tsp dried thyme

1 tbsp toasted sesame seeds

1 tbsp finely chopped marjoram leaves

1 tbsp finely chopped oregano

a good sprinkle of coarse sea salt

1 To make the za'atar, grind all the ingredients together in a mortar and pestle or small blender to make a coarse powder. Store in an airtight container until ready to use. It keeps well for 1 month.

2 To prepare the squid, hold the body with one hand and the head with the other. Gently pull the head away from the body, taking the milky white intestines with it.

3 Remove the tentacles by cutting them off just in front of the eyes. If the tentacles are large, cut into a few pieces. Discard the head.

4 Cut the body of the squid open down one side, flatten it and scrape out the guts, then, with a serrated knife, score parallel lines 1cm (½in) apart along the inner side of the flattened body. Repeat at right angles to the first score lines to make a criss-cross effect. Take care not to cut right through.

5 Place the squid pieces and tentacles in a bowl, drizzle over the oil and season with salt and pepper to taste.

6 Heat a ribbed griddle over a high heat until hot and slightly smoking. Place the squid on the griddle together with the chorizo slices and cherry tomatoes and grill for 2–3 minutes, turning occasionally until lightly charred and softened.

7 Meanwhile, make the dressing. Mix the lemon juice, sherry vinegar, garlic, chilli, oil and fennel seeds in a bowl and season to taste.

8 Add the cooked squid, chorizo and tomatoes together with the rocket, parsley and olives. Toss gently together and divide between 4 serving plates. Sprinkle over 1 tsp of the za'atar and serve immediately.

It's vitally important to cook the squid quickly on a hot ribbed griddle to retain its tenderness. The saltiness of the chorizo adds great flavour to this dish. Za'atar is a Middle-Eastern condiment blend that's used on meats, fish, vegetables, rice and bread. In other words, it's extremely versatile.

Leek and potato salad
with hot Toulouse sausage dressing

The dressing for this simple salad needs to be a little sharp in flavour and for the salad to be enjoyed at its best, you should add the sausages hot, straight from the grill.

325g (11oz) waxy salad potatoes

12 young leeks, washed, trimmed and cut into 5cm (2in) lengths

pinch of caster sugar

4 plum tomatoes, cut into wedges

2 tbsp coarsely chopped flat-leaf parsley

4 Little Gem lettuces, leaves separated and torn into small pieces

1 oakleaf lettuce, leaves separated and torn into small pieces

4 Toulouse sausages (see p.32)

vegetable oil, for brushing

salt and freshly ground black pepper

FOR THE DRESSING

1 garlic clove, peeled and bruised

1 large shallot, finely chopped

1 tbsp Dijon mustard

1 tbsp red wine vinegar

2 tbsp olive oil

2 tbsp clear honey

salt and freshly ground black pepper

1 Put the unpeeled potatoes in a pan of lightly salted water, bring to the boil, reduce the heat and cook for 20 minutes, or until they are just tender. Allow to cool slightly before peeling and cutting into 1cm (½in) slices.

2 Meanwhile, put the leeks in a pan of water with a little sugar. Bring to the boil, reduce the heat and cook for 2–3 minutes, or until they are just tender. Drain and leave to cool.

3 Place the leeks and potatoes in a bowl, add the tomatoes, parsley and lettuce, and set aside.

4 To make the dressing, rub the bruised garlic clove around the interior of a small bowl. Add the shallot, mustard and vinegar and mix well. Whisk in the olive oil, honey and 2 tbsp of cold water. Season with salt and pepper to taste, and set aside.

5 Meanwhile, heat a ribbed griddle over a high heat until hot and slightly smoking. Brush the sausages with a little vegetable oil, place on the griddle and cook, turning regularly for 15–20 minutes, or until golden all over and cooked through. Transfer the cooked sausages to a chopping board, cut into small dice, then quickly add to the bowl of salad. Pour over the shallot vinaigrette, toss well, divide the salad between 4 serving plates, and serve immediately.

Venison sausage salad with oranges

This is a tasty salad to enjoy during the game season or at any time for that matter. If you like, you can replace the venison sausages with other game sausages; the salad will still be delicious.

1 tbsp vegetable oil

6 venison sausages (see p.41)

1 large head of frisée lettuce, washed and well drained

120g (scant 4½oz) baby spinach leaves, washed and well dried

2 oranges, peeled and cut into slices or segments, to garnish (juice reserved)

1 medium red onion, thinly sliced, to garnish

50g (1¾oz) hazelnuts, lightly toasted, to garnish

FOR THE DRESSING
4 tbsp thick balsamic vinegar
reserved orange juice (see above)
1 tbsp brown sugar
½ tsp Dijon mustard
2 tbsp good-quality olive oil
1 tsp hazelnut oil

1 Heat the vegetable oil in a frying pan over a medium heat. Add the sausages and cook for 15–20 minutes, stirring occasionally until golden all over. Remove to a plate with a slotted spoon. Cover the plate with tinfoil to keep warm.

2 To make the dressing, boil together the balsamic vinegar, reserved orange juice and sugar for 1 minute in a small pan. Pour into a bowl and leave to cool, then add the mustard, 100ml (3½fl oz) of cold water, and the olive and hazelnut oils. Whisk together well.

3 Place the frisée and spinach leaves in a bowl, spoon over the dressing and toss together well.

4 Divide the salad between 4 serving plates and garnish with the oranges, onion and toasted hazelnuts. Cut the venison sausages into 10cm (4in) slices, scatter over the salad and serve immediately.

pasta and rice

Pappardelle with
venison sausage ragù

The great ragùs – sauces – of Italy are well known for the wide range of tasty meat that they incorporate, from game to offal. To accompany a ragù, you need good-quality pasta. This recipe uses fresh pappardelle – large, very broad noodles – but any type of fresh or dried noodle pasta can be used. Passata is a smooth tomato sauce that can be bought in most stores and supermarkets.

3 tbsp olive oil

8 venison sausages (see p.41), cut into 2.5cm (1in) dice

2 shallots, finely chopped

1 garlic clove, crushed

150g (5½oz) button mushrooms, thinly sliced

100ml (3½fl oz) red wine

150ml (¼ pint) chicken stock

150ml (¼ pint) passata

¼ tsp dried red chilli flakes

2 anchovy fillets, finely chopped

6 sage leaves, finely chopped

500g (1lb 2oz) fresh pappardelle or other noodle pasta

25g (scant 1oz) unsalted butter

2 tbsp finely grated Pecorino or Parmesan

grated nutmeg

salt and freshly ground black pepper

1 Heat 2 tbsp of the oil in a frying pan. Add the sausages and, taking care not to break them, cook over a medium heat for 3–4 minutes, stirring occasionally until golden. Add the shallots, garlic and mushrooms, and cook for 2 minutes more.

2 Pour over the wine and bring to the boil. Add the stock, passata, chilli, anchovy and sage, reduce the heat and simmer for 10 minutes.

3 Meanwhile, cook the pappardelle in a large pan of boiling salted water, following the packet instructions, until al dente. Drain well, toss with the butter and cheese, then season with a little nutmeg and salt and pepper to taste.

4 Divide the cooked pasta between 4 serving bowls, spoon over the sausage ragù, drizzle over the remaining oil and serve immediately.

Taglierini with kale and hot sausage sauce

Taglierini are a type of ribbon pasta. They are similar to tagliatelle, but a little narrower. You can substitute any other ribbon pasta if you like.

2 tbsp olive oil

6 hot Italian sausages (see p.36), cut into small pieces

1 medium onion, finely chopped

300g (11oz) curly kale, trimmed and finely shredded

100ml (3½fl oz) dry white wine

400g (14oz) tin peeled and chopped plum tomatoes

1 tsp coarsely chopped oregano

12 basil leaves

450g (1lb) taglierini, fresh or dried

salt and freshly ground black pepper

50g (1¾oz) Pecorino, finely grated, to serve

1 Heat the oil in a frying pan. Add the sausages and cook over a medium heat for 8–10 minutes, stirring occasionally until they are golden brown.

2 Add the onion and kale and cook for 4–5 minutes, until wilted, then add the wine and bring to the boil.

3 Add the tomatoes and cook for 6–8 minutes, until the sauce thickens, then stir in the oregano and basil. Season with salt and pepper to taste, then reduce the heat and cover with a lid to keep warm.

4 Meanwhile, cook the taglierini in a large pan of boiling salted water, following the packet instructions, until al dente. Drain well.

5 Mix the cooked pasta with the sauce, then divide between 4 serving bowls. Sprinkle with grated Pecorino and serve immediately.

Penne and fennel-crumbled Italian sausage

This dish is similar to one I ate on holiday in Rome some years ago. Penne are ribbed, tube-shaped pasta that are readily available. Luganega is a mild coiled sausage that's made throughout Italy. In the south of the country they often make it with some chilli to give it a little more kick.

300g (11oz) luganega sausage, skin removed and cut into 1cm (½in) dice

1 garlic clove, crushed

1 large head of fennel and its fronds, trimmed and cut into 1cm (½in) dice

2 tbsp Pernod or other aniseed liqueur

100ml (3½fl oz) chicken stock

¼ tsp dried red chilli flakes, to taste

450g (1lb) penne pasta

50ml (scant 2fl oz) double cream

salt and freshly ground black pepper

1 Heat a non-stick frying pan over a medium heat. Add the sausage and fry, stirring occasionally for 5–8 minutes, until the sausage is golden-brown.

2 Add the garlic and cook for 1 minute more, stirring, then add the fennel together with the Pernod and stock. Reduce the heat and cook for 10 minutes, or until the fennel is tender. Season with salt, pepper and chilli flakes to taste.

3 Meanwhile, cook the penne in a large pan of boiling salted water, following the packet instructions, until al dente. Drain well.

4 Add the cooked pasta to the sausage and fennel mix, then add the cream. Toss together and heat gently for a minute to warm through, then transfer to 4 serving dishes and serve immediately.

Rigatoni with chorizo and scallops

Sweet sea scallops are delicious when paired with spicy foods and in this recipe I combine them with chorizo. The result is a simple but extremely satisfying dish.

2 tbsp olive oil

1 garlic clove, crushed

125g (4½oz) chorizo picante (see p.32), skin removed and cut into small dice

8 large sea scallops, removed from the shell, cleaned and each cut into 4 pieces

250g (9oz) red cherry tomatoes, coarsely chopped

¼ tsp dried red chilli flakes

3 tbsp coarsely chopped flat-leaf parsley

450g (1lb) rigatoni pasta

salt and freshly ground black pepper

1 Heat the oil in a frying pan over a medium heat. Add the garlic and cook, stirring, for 30 seconds, until softened.

2 Add the chorizo, increase the heat and sauté for 2 minutes, until the fat in the sausage begins to melt. Add the scallops and cook for 1 minute more.

3 Add the tomatoes, chilli flakes and flat-leaf parsley, then reduce the heat and cover with a lid to keep warm.

4 Meanwhile, cook the rigatoni in a large pan of boiling salted water, following the packet instructions, until al dente. Drain well.

5 Combine the chorizo, scallops and pasta and season with salt and pepper to taste. Serve immediately in 4 bowls.

Penne and fennel-crumbled Italian sausage

Orecchiette with chorizo,
pecorino and pangrattato

Orecchiette are a distinctive type of pasta from Puglia. They are shaped roughly like small ears, hence their Italian name meaning 'little ears'. Pangrattato is a crispy breadcrumb mix that is quite widely used as a topping in Italian cookery.

2 tbsp olive oil

125g (4½oz) chorizo picante (see p.32) or hot Italian sausage (see p.36), skin removed and cut into small dice

100ml (3½fl oz) dry white wine

¼ tsp dried red chilli flakes

4 large plum tomatoes, halved, deseeded and cut into small dice

12 basil leaves, torn into small pieces

400g (14oz) orecchiette pasta

75g (2½oz) Pecorino, finely grated

FOR THE PANGRATTATO

90ml (scant 3½fl oz) olive oil

1 garlic clove, crushed

75g (2½oz) fresh white breadcrumbs

salt and freshly ground black pepper

1 Heat the oil in a frying pan over a medium heat. Add the chorizo and cook for 2–3 minutes, stirring occasionally until golden. Remove with a slotted spoon and set aside.

2 Add the wine to the pan, increase the heat and bring to the boil. Add the chilli flakes, tomatoes and basil, reduce the heat and keep warm.

3 Meanwhile, cook the orecchiette in a large pan of boiling salted water, following the packet instructions, until al dente. Drain, reserving 100ml (3½fl oz) of the cooking liquid.

4 Return the cooked pasta to the pan and add the reserved cooking liquid, wine and tomato sauce. Cook for 1 minute over a medium heat.

5 Meanwhile, prepare the pangratatto. Heat the oil in a frying pan over a medium heat. Add the garlic and breadcrumbs and fry, stirring occasionally for about 2 minutes, until golden and crispy. Season with salt and pepper to taste and stir in half the Pecorino.

6 Divide the pasta and sauce between 4 serving bowls, sprinkle with remaining Pecorino and serve immediately, sprinkled with the pangrattato.

Baked penne and baduzzi with young nettles

Baduzzi is the name given to small veal meatballs made in Sicily and flavoured with Pecorino and parsley. I use pork and herb sausages instead of veal. To my mind, they are just as good. Traditionally served in a broth, here they are tossed with penne pasta and young, wilted nettles before being baked 'al forno' – in the oven. Remember to wear gloves when picking your nettles to avoid being stung.

100g (3½oz) chopped nettles

8 pork and herb sausages (see p.30), skin removed

1 free-range egg, beaten

50g (1¾oz) Pecorino, finely grated, plus 2 tbsp for sprinkling

150g (5½oz) fresh white breadcrumbs

2 tbsp coarsely chopped flat-leaf parsley

2 tbsp olive oil

1 garlic clove, crushed

150ml (¼ pint) dry white wine

400g (14oz) tin peeled and chopped plum tomatoes

1 tsp caster sugar

50g (1¾oz) ground almonds

5 cups (400g) penne pasta

salt and freshly ground black pepper

1 Blanch the nettles in boiling water for 30 seconds, then drain well and set aside.

2 Place the sausages in a bowl and mix well with the egg, Pecorino, breadcrumbs and parsley. Season with salt and pepper to taste, chill in the fridge for 1 hour, then, using wet hands, roll into small balls, about 2.5cm (1in) in diameter. Set aside.

3 Preheat the oven to 180°C (350°F/Gas 4).

4 Heat the oil in a frying pan over a medium heat. Add the meatballs and garlic, and fry for 8–10 minutes, stirring occasionally until evenly browned.

5 Add the wine, cook for 2 minutes more, then add the tomatoes, sugar, nettles and almonds. Reduce the heat and simmer for 8–10 minutes, until thoroughly cooked through.

6 Meanwhile, cook the penne in a large pan of boiling salted water, following the packet instructions, until al dente. Drain well.

7 Mix together the meatballs and sauce and the cooked pasta, then season to taste.

8 Transfer to an ovenproof dish, sprinkle over the remaining Pecorino and bake in the preheated oven for 5–6 minutes, or until the cheese is golden and bubbly. Allow to cool slightly before serving.

Farro risotto with luganega
and porcini mushrooms

Farro is a type of Italian barley that has been popular in Italy since Roman times. It is usually cooked in soups or served as an accompaniment to main meals. You can find it in Italian delis, but you could substitute pearl barley if you want. You could also use button mushrooms instead of porcini, but of course the flavour will be less earthy.

50g (1¾oz) unsalted butter

1 tbsp olive oil

1 medium onion, finely chopped

400g (14oz) luganega sausage, cut into small pieces

½ tsp fennel seeds

250g (9oz) fresh porcini or button mushrooms, thickly sliced

½ tsp finely chopped thyme leaves

200g (7oz) farro or rinsed pearl barley

100ml (3½fl oz) dry white wine

750ml (1¼ pints) vegetable or chicken stock

25g (scant 1oz) Parmesan, finely grated

salt and freshly ground black pepper

shavings of Parmesan, to serve

1 Melt half the butter with the oil in a pan over a medium heat. Add the onion and cook for 2 minutes, stirring occasionally until it begins to soften.

2 Add the sausage and fennel seeds, fry for 2–3 minutes, stirring occasionally until the sausage is sealed, then remove the sausages with a slotted spoon and set aside.

3 Increase the heat, add the sliced porcini or button mushrooms and thyme, and fry for 2–3 minutes, stirring, until golden.

4 Add the farro or barley. Cook for 1 minute more to coat the grains with the oil, then add the wine and stir.

5 Meanwhile, bring the stock to the boil in another pan, then reduce the heat to keep the stock gently simmering.

6 Start adding the stock to the farro, a ladleful at a time, stirring constantly until the stock is absorbed and the farro is tender, about 20–25 minutes.

7 Return the sausage to the pan during the last 5 minutes of cooking, then stir in the Parmesan and the remaining butter until the mixture is thick and creamy.

8 Adjust the seasoning and serve immediately in 4 bowls, garnished with shavings of Parmesan.

Minted pea and spinach risotto
with sausage balls

This dish makes a delicious and satisfying main course. I love its vibrant green colour. I use traditional lamb and mint sausages here, but other types of sausage will work just as well.

200g (7oz) spinach leaves, stems removed

2 tbsp olive oil

1 small onion, finely chopped

1 garlic clove, crushed

800ml (scant 1½ pints) chicken or vegetable stock

250g (9oz) risotto rice (such as arborio, vialone nano or carnaroli)

120g (scant 4½oz) fresh shelled or frozen peas

50g (1¾oz) unsalted butter

2 tbsp finely grated Parmesan

1 tsp grated lemon zest

2 tbsp coarsely chopped mint leaves

2 tbsp prepared basil pesto

salt and freshly ground black pepper

2 tbsp basil cress, to garnish (optional)

FOR THE SAUSAGE BALLS

200g (7oz) lamb and mint sausages (see p.39), skin removed

1 Bring a large pan of salted water to the boil. Add the spinach and blanch for 1 minute. Remove and refresh in iced water. Drain and squeeze out the excess moisture, then chop finely and set aside.

2 Heat half the oil in a heavy-based pan over a medium heat. Add the onion and garlic. Reduce the heat and cook gently for 5–6 minutes, stirring occasionally until the onion is softened.

3 Meanwhile, bring the stock to the boil in another pan, then reduce the heat to keep the stock gently simmering.

4 Add the rice to the onion and garlic mixture and stir well to coat the rice with the oil.

5 Add 200ml (7fl oz) of the boiling stock to the rice and stir well. Cook, stirring occasionally until the rice has completely absorbed the stock, then add another 200ml (7fl oz) of boiling stock. Continue adding the stock gradually until the rice is almost cooked and creamy.

6 Add the chopped spinach and peas, then stir in the butter, half the Parmesan, the lemon zest, mint and pesto. Season with salt and pepper to taste.

7 Meanwhile, form the sausage meat into small marble-sized balls with wetted hands. Season with salt and pepper to taste.

8 Heat the remaining oil in a large non-stick frying pan and fry the sausage balls for 2–3 minutes, stirring occasionally until cooked and golden.

9 Divide the risotto between 4 plates or shallow bowls. Top with the sausage balls and sprinkle over the remaining Parmesan. Garnish with the basil cress, if using, and serve immediately.

Sausage and soft-egg biryani

Biryani is an Indian rice-based dish made with basmati rice and spices mixed with meat, fish and hard-boiled eggs. Here I use soft-boiled eggs, which ooze over the rice when cut. The name 'biryani' derives from the Persian word 'beryan', meaning fried or roasted.

2 tbsp vegetable oil

275g (9½oz) shallots or onions, thinly sliced

1 garlic clove, crushed

2.5cm (1in) piece of root ginger, finely chopped

200ml (7fl oz) natural yoghurt

25g (scant 1oz) ghee or clarified butter

1 tsp whole cumin seeds

10 whole cloves

10 black or green cardamom pods, lightly toasted

2 cinnamon sticks

1 bay leaf

50g (1¾oz) sultanas

450g (1lb) lamb and mint sausages (see p.39), cut into small pieces

300g (11oz) good-quality basmati rice, soaked in water for 30 minutes then drained

generous pinch of saffron strands or powdered saffron

4 free-range eggs

1 tsp salt

coriander leaves, to garnish

1 Heat the oil in a high-sided frying pan. When the oil is hot, add the shallots or onions and fry, stirring occasionally until golden. Remove with a slotted spoon onto kitchen paper to drain thoroughly.

2 In a mortar, crush the garlic, ginger and yoghurt to a smooth paste. Set aside.

3 Melt the ghee or clarified butter in a pan over a medium heat. Add the cumin, cloves, cardamom, cinnamon, bay leaf and sultanas, and cook, stirring, for 1 minute. Add the sausage pieces and mix well.

4 Add the prepared rice and the garlic, ginger and yoghurt paste, together with 500ml (17fl oz) of boiling water and 1 tsp of salt. Increase the heat, bring to the boil, stir once and cover with a tight-fitting lid. Reduce the heat and simmer for 10 minutes, until the rice is almost cooked through.

5 Meanwhile, mix the saffron in a bowl with 3 tbsp of boiling water. Leave to infuse for 2 minutes, then uncover the rice, drizzle over the saffron water, cover again, then remove from the heat. Leave to stand, covered, for 5 minutes.

6 Meanwhile, cook the eggs in simmering water for 4 minutes, until soft-boiled. Remove with a slotted spoon and leave to cool for 1 minute before peeling.

7 Uncover the rice, gently fluff up with a fork and transfer to a serving dish or individual plates. Cut the soft-boiled eggs in half. Scatter over the crispy fried shallots, top with the eggs and serve immediately, garnished with fresh coriander.

Merguez with tomatoes, peppers and green couscous

Who would have thought that couscous, from the Maghreb in North Africa, would become so widely available in the West and so popular in such a short space of time? Much of its popularity might be down to the fact that it cooks quickly and is a healthy choice.

generous handful of mint leaves

generous handful of coriander leaves

generous handful of flat-leaf parsley

2 garlic cloves, crushed

2 tbsp olive oil

450g (1lb) mini merguez sausages (see p.38) or other small fresh spicy sausages

290g (10½oz) jar roasted red peppers, drained, deseeded and cut into strips

1 tsp ground cumin

1 tbsp harissa paste

150g (5½oz) red cherry tomatoes

150g (5½oz) yellow cherry tomatoes

50g (1¾oz) dry pitted black olives

325g (11oz) couscous

450ml (¾ pint) chicken stock

30g (1oz) flaked almonds, toasted

salt and freshly ground black pepper

1 Preheat the oven to 200°C (400°F/Gas 6).

2 Put the mint, coriander and parsley in a small blender with 100ml (3½fl oz) of water and half the garlic. Blitz until smooth and set aside.

3 Heat the oil over a medium heat in a wide, deep flameproof casserole. Add the sausages and fry for 2–3 minutes, stirring occasionally until evenly browned. Remove with a slotted spoon, and set aside.

4 Add the peppers, remaining garlic, cumin and harissa to the casserole, and fry for 2 minutes more, then return the sausages to the casserole, add the cherry tomatoes and olives, and scatter the couscous over the top.

5 Put the stock in a pan, bring to the boil, then reduce the heat.

6 Mix the blended herb purée with the hot stock, pour over the couscous, stir gently, then cover the casserole. Place in the preheated oven.

7 Stir after 10 minutes, return to the oven and cook for 5 minutes more, then fluff up the couscous with a fork. Scatter over the almonds, adjust the seasoning and serve immediately.

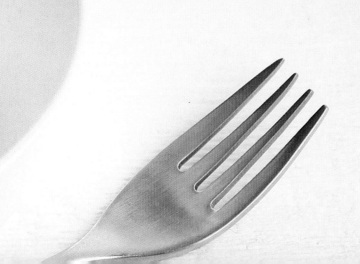

fried and grilled

Creole barbecue sausages
with grilled vegetables and salsa criolla

These sausages are terrific with any grilled vegetables. Simply choose your favourites – baby carrots, onion quarters, baby corn and squash all work well – grill them, add the sausages, spoon over the salsa criolla, and off you go!

½ tsp ground cumin

1 tsp sweet paprika

2 tsp salt

½ tsp garlic powder

½ tsp dried thyme

½ tsp dried oregano

¼ tsp ground black pepper

pinch of cayenne pepper

8–12 Oxford sausages (see p.34)

2 tbsp olive oil

your choice of vegetables

salt and freshly ground black pepper

FOR THE SALSA CRIOLLA

2 plum tomatoes, peeled, deseeded and cut into small dice

½ medium onion, coarsely chopped

1 garlic clove, crushed

1 red chilli, deseeded and finely chopped

3 tbsp red wine vinegar

1 tbsp caster sugar

3 tbsp coarsely chopped coriander leaves

2 tbsp vegetable oil

salt and freshly ground black pepper

1 For the salsa criolla, mix all the ingredients together in a small bowl, season with salt and pepper to taste, and set aside.

2 Put the cumin, paprika, salt, garlic powder, thyme, oregano, black pepper and cayenne pepper in a bowl and mix together.

3 Brush the sausages with the olive oil, then dip in the spice and herb mixture.

4 Heat two ribbed griddles over a medium to high heat until hot and slightly smoking. Add your choice of prepared vegetables to one griddle and grill for 10–15 minutes, turning occasionally until lightly charred and tender. Season with salt and pepper to taste.

5 Add the seasoned sausages to the second griddle and cover with a piece of tinfoil. Cook for 15–20 minutes, lifting the tinfoil and turning the sausages occasionally until cooked through.

6 Put the sausages on a bed of the grilled vegetables, spoon over some salsa criolla and serve immediately.

Chinese sausages
with bok choy and water chestnuts

Lap cheong are dried, highly seasoned Chinese sausages that are usually smoked. They have a pronounced sweetness. The best way to prepare them is to poach them or, as in this recipe, to blanch them. Then you can add them to the stir-fry. Lap cheong sausages are available from Chinese stores. They're usually vacuum-packed and must be refrigerated after opening. If you prefer, you can use any country pork sausages instead. I like to serve this dish on top of a pile of hot sticky rice.

450g (1lb) lap cheong or country pork sausages (see p.30)

2 tbsp sunflower or peanut oil

6 spring onions, trimmed and cut into 2.5cm (1in) lengths

2 garlic cloves, thinly sliced

5cm (2in) piece of root ginger, peeled and cut into thin strips

4 baby bok choy, cut into quarters

1 tbsp Shaoxing wine or dry sherry

2 tbsp kecap manis or light soy sauce

150ml (¼ pint) oyster sauce

100ml (3½fl oz) chicken stock

100g (3½oz) tinned water chestnuts, drained and thinly sliced

1 Blanch the sausages in a pan of boiling water for 2 minutes, until they are opaque. Drain, leave to cool, then slice thinly and set aside.

2 Heat the oil in a wok or large frying pan over a high heat. Add the spring onions, garlic and ginger and stir-fry for 2 minutes.

3 Add the sliced sausages and bok choy and stir-fry for 1 minute more.

4 Add the wine, kecap manis, oyster sauce and chicken stock and stir-fry for 2–3 minutes more.

5 Add the water chestnuts then serve immediately.

Jambalaya stir-fry

New Orleans is the home of jambalaya, a rice dish made with spicy sausage, ham and prawns. It's seasoned with hot cayenne pepper and sweetened with peppers, tomatoes and garlic. Here's my quick, stir-fry variation using chorizo. Some may regard this as heresy, but it's delicious and quickly put together.

2 tbsp sunflower oil

250g (9oz) chorizo picante (see p.32), merguez (see p.38) or Cajun andouille sausages (see p.33), skin removed and cut into 2.5cm (1in) slices

350g (12oz) raw tiger prawns, peeled and deveined

1 tsp paprika

1 small green pepper, halved, deseeded and coarsely chopped

1 small red pepper, halved, deseeded and coarsely chopped

1 garlic clove, crushed

2 sticks celery, trimmed and thinly sliced

450g (1lb) cooked white long-grain rice

2 tbsp hot chilli sauce

1 tsp finely chopped thyme leaves

1 tsp finely chopped oregano

4 spring onions, trimmed and thinly sliced

cayenne pepper

salt and freshly ground black pepper

1 Heat the oil in a large frying pan over a medium heat. Add the chorizo slices and prawns, and fry for 2 minutes, stirring occasionally until golden.
2 Add the paprika, peppers, garlic and celery, and cook for 4–5 minutes, stirring occasionally until lightly browned.
3 Add the cooked rice and mix together well. Stir in the chilli sauce, herbs and spring onions, and cook for 2 minutes more, stirring occasionally.
4 Season with salt, pepper and cayenne pepper to taste. Serve immediately.

Flash-fried black pudding
with sage-creamed cabbage and apple chutney

Many people see black pudding as a breakfast staple, but in fact, it makes a tasty main-course dish. The combination of black pudding with cabbage is to die for. The accompanying apple chutney is easy to make if you follow my recipe on page 186.

800g (1¾lb) floury potatoes (such as King Edward or Desirée)

100ml (3½fl oz) full-fat milk

150ml (¼ pint) double cream

100g (3½oz) unsalted butter

½ tbsp prepared English mustard

1 medium Savoy cabbage, trimmed and finely shredded

4 sage leaves, torn

4 black pudding rings, skin removed and cut into thick slices

salt and freshly ground black pepper

150ml (¼ pint) apple chutney (see p.186), to serve

1 Peel the potatoes and cut them into large chunks. Put in a pan of lightly salted water, bring to the boil, reduce the heat and cook for 25 minutes, or until tender. Drain well, then mash with a potato masher or pass through a potato ricer. Set aside.

2 Put the milk, 50ml (scant 2fl oz) of cream and half the butter in a small clean pan. Warm over a medium heat, then beat into the mashed potatoes. Add the mustard and return the mash to its pan. Cover the pan to keep the mash warm.

3 Put the cabbage in a pan of boiling water over a medium heat and cook for 5–6 minutes. Remove from the heat and drain well.

4 Return the cabbage to its pan, add the remaining cream and the sage, and cook over a low heat for 2–3 minutes, stirring, until the cream has reduced to a thick sauce that binds the cabbage. Season with salt and pepper to taste.

5 Meanwhile, put the remaining butter in a frying pan over a medium heat. When the butter is hot, add the sliced black pudding and fry gently for 5 minutes, turning occasionally. Season with salt and pepper to taste.

6 Divide the creamed cabbage between 4 serving plates, top with black pudding, place the mustard mash alongside, and serve with the apple chutney.

White pudding with shallots
and wild mushrooms

In this dish, the white pudding and salsa verde – or green sauce – really pull together the flavours of the earthy wild mushrooms and the shallot garnish. I often serve this over a bed of polenta or creamy mash.

8 large banana shallots

8 thick slices of white pudding (see p.33), about 2.5cm (1in) thick

1 tbsp olive oil

400g (14oz) wild mushrooms, cleaned and trimmed

1 tsp finely chopped thyme leaves

salt and freshly ground black pepper

125ml (4fl oz) salsa verde (see p.185), to serve

1 Blanch the shallots in a pan of boiling water for 4–5 minutes, then remove and leave to cool. When cool enough to handle, peel carefully, then cut in half lengthways, keeping the root intact to stop the layers from falling apart. Set aside.

2 Meanwhile, heat a ribbed griddle over a medium heat until hot and slightly smoking. Brush the white pudding slices liberally with oil, then put them on the griddle. Cook for 10–12 minutes, turning regularly until they are golden and cooked through. Alternatively, pan-fry the white pudding in olive oil. Remove to a plate and cover with tinfoil to keep warm.

3 Toss the mushrooms and shallots together in a bowl then scatter on the hot griddle. Add the thyme, season with a little salt and pepper and grill for 8–10 minutes, until golden, keeping them moving as they cook.

4 Divide the white pudding, mushrooms and shallots between 4 serving plates. Spoon the salsa verde over the white pudding and serve immediately.

Polpettone with egg, capers
and anchovy pan sauce

Polpettone are tiny fritters or rissoles that are popular in Italy. The Parmesan breadcrumbs add great texture, but for best results, make sure you fry the polpettone until they're crisp and golden. Sauté potatoes and spinach, cooked in a little butter until tender, seasoned with salt, pepper and a grating of nutmeg, make an ideal accompaniment to this dish. Delicious!

300g (11oz) floury potatoes
(such as Maris Piper or Desirée)

4 tbsp plain flour

1 free-range egg yolk, plus extra beaten egg for dipping

30g (1oz) Parmesan, finely grated

5 tbsp olive oil

6 Cumberland sausages (see p.31), skin removed

1 shallot, finely chopped

45g (1½oz) fresh white breadcrumbs

45g (1½oz) Pecorino, finely grated

50g (1¾oz) salted butter

2 tbsp baby capers, rinsed and dried

2 tbsp coarsely chopped flat-leaf parsley

2 anchovy fillets in oil, drained
and finely chopped

juice of ½ lemon

4 free-range eggs

salt and freshly ground black pepper

1 Put the unpeeled potatoes in a pan of lightly salted water, bring to the boil, reduce the heat and simmer for 20 minutes, until tender. Drain well and leave to cool. When cool enough to handle, peel, then return to the pan.

2 Add half the flour and mash with a potato masher or pass through a potato ricer until smooth. Return the pan to the heat, add the egg yolk and Parmesan, mix well and leave to cool.

3 Meanwhile, heat 2 tbsp of olive oil in a frying pan over a medium heat. Add the sausages and fry for 15–20 minutes, stirring occasionally and breaking them up with a fork as they cook.

4 Add the shallot, cook for 5 minutes, then remove the sausage and shallot with a slotted spoon. Leave to cool.

5 Once cool, mix the potato with the sausage and shallot in a bowl. Season with salt and pepper to taste.

6 In another bowl, combine the breadcrumbs and the Pecorino.

7 Shape the potato and sausage mixture into 8 equal-size patties, then pass first through the remaining flour, then through the beaten egg, and finally through the breadcrumb mix.

8 Heat the remaining oil in a large non-stick frying pan over a medium heat. Add the patties and fry for 7–8 minutes on each side until golden. Remove with a slotted spoon onto kitchen paper to drain, then put on a plate and cover with tinfoil to keep warm.

9 Add the butter to this frying pan and when it begins to foam, add the capers, parsley and anchovy. Squeeze over the lemon juice.

10 Heat the remaining 3 tbsp of olive oil in a small clean frying pan over a medium heat. Add 1 or 2 eggs at a time and fry, sunny side up.

11 To serve, place 2 patties on each serving plate, accompany with a fried egg and spoon over the pan sauce.

Rosemary grilled sausages
with balsamic chocolate caponata

This is a simple flavour-packed dish. Caponata is a sweet-and-sour Italian relish, which can be eaten hot or cold as a starter. In Italy many recipes for it include chocolate and balsamic vinegar, so when I discovered balsamic chocolate vinegar, I just had to try it. I'm pleased to say, it works beautifully. I suggest serving some diced potatoes crisply roasted in olive oil as an accompaniment.

8–12 country pork (see p.30) or lamb sausages (see p.39)

12 large sprigs of rosemary

2 tbsp olive oil

salt and freshly ground black pepper

FOR THE CAPONATA

2 tbsp olive oil

2 large aubergines, cut into 2.5cm (1in) dice

2 sticks celery, trimmed and cut into 2.5cm (1in) dice

1 medium onion, finely chopped

200g (7oz) tin peeled plum tomatoes

1 tbsp caster sugar

12 pitted green olives

50g (1¾oz) pine nuts

45g (1½oz) baby capers, rinsed and dried

100ml (3½fl oz) chocolate balsamic vinegar

1 tbsp finely grated dark chocolate

1 For the caponata, put the olive oil in a large frying pan over a high heat. Add the aubergine and fry, stirring occasionally for 5–6 minutes, until golden. Remove with a slotted spoon onto kitchen paper to drain. Set aside. You may need to do this in batches.

2 Add the celery to the pan, adding a little more oil if necessary. Cook, stirring occasionally for 5 minutes, until golden, then remove with a slotted spoon onto kitchen paper to drain. Set aside.

3 Add the onion to the pan and cook, stirring occasionally for 2–3 minutes, until the onion begins to soften, then add the tomatoes and sugar, reduce the heat and simmer for 10–15 minutes.

4 Add the olives, pine nuts, capers and balsamic vinegar, then return the aubergine and celery to the pan, stir well, and simmer gently for 20 minutes.

5 Add the grated chocolate and stir until melted. Remove from the heat and cover with a lid to keep warm.

6 Meanwhile, heat a ribbed griddle over a high heat until hot and slightly smoking.

7 Skewer each sausage with a sprig of rosemary, season with salt and pepper to taste, brush with a little oil, then place on the griddle and cook for 18–20 minutes, turning regularly until golden and cooked through.

8 To serve, divide the caponata between 4 serving plates and arrange the grilled sausages on top.

Beer-battered saveloys
with crushed peas and mustard mayonnaise

For a simple mid-week treat, try this tasty sausage-based alternative to that old favourite, fish and chips. Frying the sausages in a light beer batter gives them an unmistakeable texture. In the North of England, white pudding is often cut into thick slices and fried in batter in the same way. If you like, you can try that variation. Either version is delicious with chips – as you would expect!

125g (4½oz) self-raising flour, plus extra for dusting

50g (1¾oz) cornflour

350ml (12fl oz) beer (Guinness or other malt beer)

vegetable oil, for deep-frying

8–12 saveloys or 8 thick slices of white pudding (see p.33)

salt and freshly ground black pepper

FOR THE CRUSHED PEAS

400g (14oz) peas, fresh or frozen

1 tbsp mint sauce

25g (scant 1oz) unsalted butter, chilled

salt and freshly ground black pepper

FOR THE MUSTARD MAYONNAISE

2 tsp Dijon or prepared English mustard

125ml (4fl oz) good-quality mayonnaise

1 Place the flour and cornflour in a bowl and make a well in the centre. Gradually mix in the beer to form a batter but do not over-mix. Season with salt and pepper to taste then set aside for 25 minutes.

2 Meanwhile, prepare the peas. Place the peas in a pan of boiling salted water and cook until tender. Drain well, then transfer to a blender. Add the mint sauce and the butter, then blitz until lightly crushed, using the pulse button. Return to the pan, season and cover with the lid to keep warm.

3 For the mustard mayonnaise, place the mustard and mayonnaise in a bowl and mix together thoroughly. Set aside.

4 Heat the oil to 180°C (350°F) in a deep fryer or large pan.

5 Dust each sausage in a little flour, then dip in the batter. Shake off any excess, then deep-fry in two batches for about 3–4 minutes a batch, until the sausages are cooked and the batter is crisp and golden. As each batch is ready, remove onto kitchen paper to drain.

6 Divide the sausages between 4 serving plates. Serve with crushed peas and mustard mayonnaise alongside.

My sausages and mash
with sage and onion gravy

Sausages and mash – often known as 'bangers and mash' – is one of Britain's best-loved comfort meals. You can use any country-style pork sausage but Cumberland sausages are my favourites. The sage and onion gravy is perfect to accompany the dish. It's just the job for a chilly winter's day ... or at any time for that matter!

1 tbsp olive oil or dripping

8–12 Cumberland (see p.31) or country pork sausages (see p.30)

FOR THE GRAVY

25g (scant 1oz) unsalted butter

4 medium onions, thinly sliced

1 tsp caster sugar

2 tbsp coarsely chopped sage leaves

100ml (3½fl oz) Madeira

100ml (3½fl oz) red wine

600ml (1 pint) beef stock

FOR THE MASH

625g (1lb 6oz) floury potatoes (such as Maris Piper or Desirée)

75ml (2½fl oz) full-fat milk

100ml (3½fl oz) double cream

50g (1¾oz) unsalted butter, chilled and cut into small dice

salt and freshly ground black pepper

1 For the mash, peel the potatoes and cut into large chunks. Put in a pan of lightly salted water, bring to the boil, reduce the heat and cook for 10 minutes, or until tender. Drain well and return to the pan. Mash with a potato masher or pass through a potato ricer.

2 Put the milk in a clean pan over a high heat. When hot, add to the mash with the cream and butter and beat until smooth and creamy. Season with salt and pepper to taste, then cover with a lid to keep warm.

3 Meanwhile, heat the oil or dripping in a non-stick frying pan over a medium heat. Add the sausages. Reduce the heat to low and cook for 18–20 minutes, stirring occasionally until golden and cooked through. Remove with a slotted spoon to a plate and cover with tinfoil to keep warm.

4 For the gravy, add the butter to the frying pan, then add the onions and sugar. Fry over a low heat for 8–10 minutes, stirring occasionally until the onions are golden and caramelised.

5 Stir in the sage, Madeira, red wine and stock, increase the heat and bring to the boil. Reduce the heat and simmer for 7–8 minutes, until the liquid has reduced by two-thirds.

6 To serve, pile the creamy mashed potatoes onto 4 serving plates. Top with the sausages and pour over the gravy.

Sausage saltimbocca
with sage and ricotta

Saltimbocca is Italian for 'jumps in the mouth'. I can only imagine it refers to the 'jump' of flavour that you get when you eat it. It's traditionally made from thin tender slices of veal and prosciutto cooked with sage and served with a sauce made from the pan juices and a little lemon. Some recipes suggest using a Marsala sauce. I think sausages make an extremely good alternative to the veal. My version also includes a little ricotta cheese. This is a dish you never get tired of eating. I like to serve it with some sweet potato mash and buttered cavolo nero (Italian black cabbage) or spinach.

12 slices of prosciutto

50g (1¾oz) good-quality ricotta cheese

12 sage leaves

12 Cumberland (see p.31) or mild Italian sausages (see p.36)

2 tbsp olive oil

45g (1½oz) salted butter

juice of ¼ lemon

FOR THE CAPER-WALNUT SAUCE

12 walnut halves

25g (scant 1oz) Parmesan, finely grated

1 garlic clove, crushed

60ml (2fl oz) olive oil

1 tbsp capers, rinsed and drained

pinch of caster sugar

1 For the caper-walnut sauce, place all the ingredients in a small blender, blitz to a coarse texture and set aside.

2 Smear each prosciutto slice lightly with 1 tbsp of ricotta cheese, then place a sage leaf and a sausage on top of each, and wrap the prosciutto round carefully to enclose the sausage.

3 Heat a frying pan over a medium heat, then add the oil. Add the sausages and cook for 18–20 minutes, turning occasionally until cooked and golden. Remove with a slotted spoon to a plate and cover with tinfoil to keep warm.

4 Add the butter to the pan and heat until it begins to foam. Add the lemon juice and remove from the heat.

5 Divide the saltimbocca between 4 serving plates, top each with some of the lemon-butter and drizzle over a little caper-walnut sauce. Serve immediately.

Short-braised faggots and kidneys
in a devilled sauce

If you love offal then you are in for a double treat. Faggots contain offal and then there are the kidneys as well. The two are quickly braised in a piquant devilled sauce. Try serving this dish with a creamy carrot purée seasoned with cumin.

8 lamb kidneys, cut in half lengthways, membrane removed

8 faggots (see p.34)

1 tbsp plain flour

2 tbsp vegetable oil

25g (scant 1oz) unsalted butter

½ tsp finely chopped thyme leaves

250g (9oz) small button onions, peeled

200g (7oz) small button mushrooms

8 whole black peppercorns, finely cracked

100ml (3½fl oz) dry white wine

4 tbsp white wine vinegar

150ml (¼ pint) veal or beef stock

2 tbsp HP sauce

cayenne pepper, salt and freshly ground black pepper, to taste

1 Season the kidneys and faggots with salt, pepper and cayenne, then pass lightly through the flour.

2 Heat the oil in a frying pan over a medium heat. Add the kidneys and faggots and fry for 6–8 minutes, turning occasionally until golden. Remove with a slotted spoon to a plate and cover with tinfoil to keep warm.

3 Add the butter, thyme and onions to the pan and fry for 5–6 minutes, stirring occasionally until golden. Add the mushrooms and fry for 2 minutes more.

4 Add the black peppercorns, wine and vinegar, increase the heat, bring to the boil and boil for 2–3 minutes, then add the stock and HP sauce and stir. Reduce the heat to a simmer.

5 Return the kidneys and faggots to the pan and simmer for 5 minutes more, until the sauce has reduced in volume by half. Serve immediately.

Sausage pitta with grilled red onions
and coriander and mint salsa

Tasty lamb and mint sausages topped with a lively little salsa and served with grilled onions make the perfect barbecue dish. Try eating just one – I dare you! Pork or beef sausages work just as well as lamb and mint if you prefer.

4 lamb and mint sausages (see p.39)

2 medium red onions, thinly sliced

4 fresh pitta breads

200g (7oz) prepared Moroccan-style hummus

100g (3½oz) mixed continental salad leaves

FOR THE SALSA

1 garlic clove, crushed

2 anchovy fillets, finely chopped

grated zest and juice of ½ lemon

100ml (3½fl oz) olive oil

generous handful of coriander leaves

generous handful of mint leaves

1 For the salsa, mix together all the ingredients in a bowl and set aside.

2 Heat a ribbed griddle over a medium heat until hot and slightly smoking. Add the sausages and cook, turning regularly for 8–10 minutes, until golden. Remove from the griddle and cut into thickish slices on the diagonal. Put on a plate and cover with tinfoil to keep warm.

3 Put the onion slices on the griddle and cook for 10 minutes, turning regularly until they are soft and golden. Remove to a plate and cover with tinfoil to keep warm.

4 Put the pitta breads on the griddle for 1 minute on each side to warm them, then remove.

5 To serve, spread the pitta breads with hummus and sprinkle over the grilled onions. Top each pitta with a handful of salad leaves, then with the slices of grilled sausage. Drizzle over the salsa and serve immediately.

Barbecue-basted sausages on succotash

Succotash is a dish from the American South made from mixed beans and corn kernels. For a fresher, cleaner taste, prepare it while your sausages are grilling. Basting the sausages with a hot, sweet and slightly soured sticky glaze, imparts a lovely flavour.

25g (scant 1oz) unsalted butter

½ tsp finely chopped thyme leaves

1 tsp prepared English mustard

2 tbsp good-quality maple syrup

2 tbsp cider vinegar or white wine vinegar

2 tbsp molasses (preferably blackstrap) or treacle

8–12 chicken sausages (see p.39)

1 tbsp vegetable oil

FOR THE SUCCOTASH
4 rashers streaky bacon, chopped

15g (½oz) unsalted butter

1 garlic clove, crushed

1 green pepper, halved, deseeded and cut into 2.5cm (1in) dice

¼ tsp finely chopped thyme leaves

200g (7oz) cooked green beans

400g (14oz) tin red kidney beans, drained and rinsed

400g (14oz) tin sweetcorn kernels, drained and rinsed

100ml (3½fl oz) chicken stock

150ml (¼ pint) double cream

4 spring onions, finely chopped

salt and freshly ground black pepper

1 Heat a ribbed griddle over a medium heat until hot and slightly smoking.

2 Meanwhile, in a small pan, bring to the boil the butter, thyme, mustard, maple syrup, vinegar and molasses.

3 Lightly brush the sausages with the oil, place on the griddle and cook for 15–20 minutes, basting them with the glaze and turning them regularly until they are cooked through.

4 Meanwhile, make the succotash. Heat a non-stick frying pan over a medium heat, add the bacon and fry until crisp and golden. Remove with a slotted spoon onto kitchen paper to drain.

5 Add the butter to the pan, followed by the garlic and pepper. Cook for 5–6 minutes, then add the thyme, green beans, kidney beans and sweetcorn. Cook together for 2–3 minutes.

6 Add the stock and cream and simmer gently until these are reduced in volume by one-third.

7 Return the bacon to the pan, add the spring onions, mix well, season with salt and pepper to taste and serve, topped with the grilled sausages.

Rosticini with polenta and
aubergine balsamic vine tomatoes

1 garlic clove, crushed

2 tbsp olive oil

½ tsp coarsely chopped thyme leaves

8–12 lamb (see p.39) or wild boar
sausages, each cut into 4 pieces

6 Japanese baby aubergines, cut into
2.5cm (1in) slices

4 tbsp good-quality thick balsamic vinegar

1 tbsp coarsely chopped marjoram

¼ tsp dried red chilli flakes

400g (14oz) cherry tomatoes on the vine

125ml (4fl oz) salsa verde (see p.185),
to serve

FOR THE POLENTA

125g (4½oz) quick-cook polenta

25g (scant 1oz) unsalted butter

2 tbsp finely grated Parmesan

salt and freshly ground black pepper

1 The day before, soak 8 wooden skewers in a bowl of water.
2 For the polenta, bring 500ml (17fl oz) of water to the boil in a pan, then
slowly add the polenta in a thin stream. Reduce the heat and cook for 10–12
minutes, stirring occasionally until the mixture thickens.
3 Remove from the heat, beat in the butter and Parmesan, and season with salt
and pepper to taste. Transfer to a greased shallow baking tin and leave to set
overnight in the fridge, covered with clingfilm.
4 Mix together the garlic, oil and thyme in a shallow dish, add the sausage
pieces, and leave to marinate overnight.
5 The next day, remove the skewers from the water and heat a ribbed griddle
over a high heat. While the griddle is heating, blanch the aubergine slices in a
pan of boiling water for 1 minute. Remove from the heat, drain and dry on a
clean tea towel. Leave to cool.
6 Remove the polenta from the fridge and cut it into large chunks or squares.
Thread alternate slices of aubergine, polenta and sausage on the skewers.
7 When the griddle is hot and slightly smoking, add the skewers and cook for
12–15 minutes, turning occasionally until the sausages are cooked through and
golden. Remove to a plate and cover with tinfoil to keep warm.
8 Meanwhile, mix the balsamic vinegar, marjoram and chilli together in a bowl.
9 Place the vine tomatoes on the griddle and cook for 4–5 minutes, basting
them with the balsamic-vinegar mixture, until they soften.
10 Divide the skewers between 4 serving dishes, top each with the glazed
tomatoes and serve immediately with the salsa verde.

Native to the Abruzzo region of Italy, traditional rosticini – also known as spiedini – are made from chunks of meat (mostly lamb), skewered like shish kebabs and quickly seared over hot coals. They are a cheap yet satisfying summer barbecue food. If you can't readily find Japanese baby aubergines, use large aubergines cut into 2.5cm (1in) dice instead.

Turkish meatballs with imam bayaldi and sumac onions

Imam bayaldi is one of Turkey's legendary dishes. It's a flavour-packed mélange of aubergine, tomatoes, peppers and onions. Although it's not strictly the correct thing to do, I like to add some spicy heat in the form of a little harissa. Sumac is a Middle-Eastern condiment with a lemony flavour that's used extensively in all manner of dishes. It's not hard to find in Middle-Eastern grocery shops.

8–12 lamb sausages (see p.39), skin removed
1 medium onion, coarsely grated
2 tsp ground cumin
½ tsp ground cinnamon
2 tbsp coarsely chopped mint
salt and freshly ground black pepper

FOR THE IMAM BAYALDI
2 aubergines, cut into 2.5cm (1in) dice
100ml (3½fl oz) olive oil
½ tsp cumin seeds
½ tsp ground cardamom
2 garlic cloves, crushed
4 plum tomatoes, coarsely chopped
2 tsp harissa paste
1 tbsp good-quality tomato ketchup
1 tbsp sultanas
2 tbsp coarsely chopped coriander leaves

FOR THE ONION RELISH
1 large red onion, thinly sliced
2 tbsp coarsely chopped mint leaves
generous sprinkle of sumac
salt and freshly ground black pepper

1 For the meatballs, place the sausage meat in a bowl, add the onion, cumin, cinnamon and mint, and mix together well. Season with salt and pepper to taste. Refrigerate for at least 2 hours.
2 For the onion relish, put all the ingredients in a bowl, mix together well and season with salt and pepper to taste. Set aside.
3 For the imam bayaldi, cook the aubergines in a pan of boiling salted water for 5–6 minutes, or until just soft. Drain well and dry in a clean tea towel. Set aside.
4 Heat the oil over a high heat in a large frying pan, add the cumin and cardamom, and cook for 1 minute, stirring constantly to release their fragrance.
5 Add the aubergine and garlic, mix together well and cook, stirring occasionally until golden.
6 Add the tomatoes, harissa, tomato ketchup and sultanas. Cook for 1 minute, then remove from the heat, stir in the coriander, and cover with a lid to keep warm.
7 Heat a ribbed griddle over a high heat until hot and slightly smoking. Add the meatballs and cook, turning occasionally for 10–15 minutes, until golden and cooked through. Serve immediately with the imam bayaldi and the onion relish.

Peppered venison sausages with wild
mushrooms, cranberries and elderberry wine sauce

Elderberry wine is a popular home-made wine, but it can also be bought. It complements the venison sausages perfectly, or the wild boar sausages if you choose to use these instead. Serve this dish with some tasty winter cabbage and crisp potato rösti.

100g (3½oz) dried cranberries

400ml (14fl oz) elderberry wine

2 tbsp vegetable oil

8–12 venison (see p.41) or wild boar sausages

1 tsp finely chopped thyme leaves

275g (9½oz) wild mushrooms, cleaned and trimmed

2 tsp cranberry jelly

2–3 juniper berries, crushed

300ml (½ pint) beef stock

1 tsp green peppercorns in brine, rinsed and dried

25g (scant 1oz) unsalted butter, chilled and cut into small dice

salt and freshly ground black pepper

1 The day before, put the cranberries and 125ml (4fl oz) of elderberry wine in a jug or bowl. Leave to soak overnight.

2 The next day, put half the oil in a large frying pan over a medium heat. Add the sausages and thyme. Fry for 15–20 minutes, stirring occasionally until golden, then remove with a slotted spoon to a plate and cover with tinfoil to keep warm.

3 Add the remaining oil to the pan, then add the wild mushrooms. Fry for 5 minutes, stirring occasionally until golden. Remove with a slotted spoon. Season with salt and pepper to taste, then set aside.

4 Put the soaked cranberries in the pan with the remaining elderberry wine, the cranberry jelly, the juniper berries and the stock. Increase the heat, bring to the boil and cook for 10 minutes, or until reduced to a syrupy consistency. Add the green peppercorns.

5 Reduce the heat, whisk in the chilled butter and season with salt and pepper to taste. Return the sausages and mushrooms to the pan and reheat gently for a couple of minutes.

6 Remove the sausages with a slotted spoon and divide between 4 serving plates. Scatter over the mushrooms and pour over the sauce to serve.

Chimichurri mixed grill

Here is a mixed grill consisting of two spicy sausages enhanced by chimichurri. This Argentinean sauce is one of my favourites. I make no apologies for using it in many of my recipe books. A sauce that's as tasty and as versatile as this one shouldn't be neglected. Note that this recipe serves 6–8 people.

1 Cumberland coil (see p.31)

1 Boerewors coil (see p.40)

2 tbsp olive oil

8 portobello mushrooms

4 firm ripe plum tomatoes, halved

a few sprigs of watercress, to garnish

FOR THE CHIMICHURRI SAUCE

40ml (1½fl oz) red wine vinegar

generous handful of flat-leaf parsley

100ml (3½fl oz) olive oil

3 garlic cloves, crushed

1 green chilli, deseeded and coarsely chopped

½ tsp dried oregano

1 For the chimichurri sauce, put the ingredients in a blender with 2 tbsp of water and blitz to a coarse paste. Remove to a bowl, cover and leave to stand for 1 hour at room temperature to allow the flavours to infuse.

2 Heat a ribbed griddle over a high heat until hot and slightly smoking.

3 Meanwhile, pierce each sausage through the middle with 2 long skewers, crossing the skewers over one another so they hold together. Brush the sausages liberally with oil, then place on the griddle together with the mushrooms and tomato halves. You may need to do this in two batches. Grill for 15–20 minutes, turning the sausages once or twice until crusty and cooked through. Occasionally turn the mushrooms and tomato halves.

4 Transfer the sausages, mushrooms and tomatoes to a serving dish and garnish with watercress. Serve with the chimichurri sauce.

Turkey sausages with
potato and smoky bacon hash

A real winter warmer, the hash that accompanies these sausages is made with a combination of two types of potato combined with spinach. It's colourful and packed with flavour. Serve with apple chutney (see page 186) on the side.

8–12 turkey sausages
2 tbsp olive oil
your choice of gravy (see p.189), to serve
apple chutney (see p.186), to serve

FOR THE HASH
300g (11oz) floury potatoes
(such as Maris Piper or Desirée)
200g (7oz) orange sweet potato
2 tbsp olive oil
4 rashers dry-cure smoky bacon,
finely chopped
1 medium onion, finely chopped
150g (5½oz) baby spinach leaves
2 tbsp coarsely chopped flat-leaf parsley
salt and freshly ground black pepper

1 For the hash, peel both types of potato and cut into 1.5cm (⅝in) dice. Put the potato and the sweet potato in separate pans of cold salted water. Bring to the boil and cook until just tender but still with a little bite. The floury potatoes will take about 20 minutes and the sweet potato will take 7–8 minutes. Drain well and set aside.

2 Heat the oil in a non-stick frying pan over a medium heat. Add the bacon and fry for 4–5 minutes, turning occasionally until crispy.

3 Add the onion and cook, stirring occasionally for 2 minutes more, until the onion begins to colour slightly. Add the spinach and cook for 1 minute more.

4 Increase the heat and add the cooked potatoes. Fry, stirring occasionally for 7–8 minutes, until the hash is golden, then add the parsley, toss together gently and season with salt and pepper to taste. Remove from the heat and cover with a lid to keep warm.

5 Meanwhile, heat a ribbed griddle over a high heat. While it is heating, brush the sausages with the oil and when the griddle is hot and slightly smoking, add the sausages. Cook, turning regularly for 18–20 minutes, until golden-brown and cooked through.

6 Serve with the potato hash, gravy and apple chutney.

oven-baked

Lincolnshire farmhouse
sausage cobbler

A cobbler is a traditional dish both in England and in America. It consists of a savoury or fruity mixture topped with a scone-like pastry dough and baked in the oven.

2 tbsp vegetable oil

8–12 Lincolnshire (see p.30) or country pork sausages (see p.30), or 400g (14oz) cocktail chipolatas

100g (3½oz) streaky bacon

1 medium onion, coarsely chopped

1 garlic clove, crushed

100g (3½oz) parsnip, peeled and diced

2 carrots, peeled and cut into 1cm (½in) slices

125g (4½oz) button or portobello mushrooms, thickly sliced

2 tbsp tomato purée

2 tbsp plain flour, plus extra for dusting

750ml (1¼ pints) beef stock

2 tbsp chopped sage leaves

1 tbsp Worcestershire sauce

FOR THE COBBLER

275g (9½oz) self-raising flour

125g (4½oz) unsalted butter, diced

50g (1¾oz) Cheddar cheese, coarsely grated

1 free-range egg, beaten

cayenne pepper, and salt and freshly ground black pepper to taste

1 Heat the oil in a large deep-sided non-stick frying pan over a medium heat. Add the sausages and bacon and fry for 5 minutes, turning occasionally. Remove with a slotted spoon and set aside.

2 Add the onion, garlic, parsnip, carrots and mushrooms to the pan and sauté for 8–10 minutes, stirring regularly until golden. Add the tomato purée and mix together well. Sprinkle over the flour and stir in well. Add the stock, chopped sage and Worcestershire sauce. Bring to the boil and stir, then cover, reduce the heat and simmer for 25–30 minutes, until the vegetables are cooked.

3 Meanwhile, preheat the oven to 190°C (375°F/Gas 5). Put the flour, butter, half the cheese, the cayenne pepper and the salt and pepper in a food processor. Process for 30 seconds, until the mixture resembles large fresh breadcrumbs, then transfer to a bowl, add 150ml (¼ pint) of cold water, and mix well.

4 Roll the dough out on a floured board to about 1cm (½in) thick. Cut into rounds with a 5cm (2in) biscuit cutter.

5 Cut the reserved sausages into 3, add to the vegetable mixture in the pan, then put in an ovenproof baking dish. Top with neatly overlapping cobbler rounds, brush with the beaten egg and bake in the preheated oven for 30 minutes, or until the topping is well risen and golden. Serve immediately.

Provençal
sausages

This tasty dish combines all the flavours of Provence. It is easy to prepare and so quick to eat! You may like to add some crumbled goat's cheese a couple of minutes before the end of cooking.

2 medium heads of fennel, trimmed and cut into 1cm (½in) wedges

1 medium red onion, cut into wedges

2 large courgettes, cut into 2.5cm (1in) thick slices

2 garlic cloves, unpeeled and halved

4 tbsp olive oil, plus a little extra for drizzling

1 tsp finely chopped thyme leaves

½ tsp finely chopped rosemary leaves

1 bay leaf

2 tbsp balsamic vinegar

400g (14oz) pork, tomato and basil sausages (see p.30)

400g (14oz) mixed red and yellow cherry tomatoes

10 basil leaves

salt and freshly ground black pepper

1 Preheat the oven to 200°C (400°F/Gas 6).

2 Put the fennel, onion, courgette and garlic in a large roasting tray. Add the oil, thyme, rosemary, bay leaf and balsamic vinegar and mix well.

3 Arrange the sausages on top, drizzle over a little oil, and season with salt and pepper to taste.

4 Place in the preheated oven and bake for 15–20 minutes, turning once or twice.

5 Add the cherry tomatoes, then tear the basil leaves and sprinkle them on top. Return to the oven for 5 minutes more. Serve immediately.

Creamy Gorgonzola polenta
with Italian sausage

Mild Italian or game sausages both give delicious results for this dish. Polenta is a popular Italian comfort food. I love flavouring it with blue cheese and, as far as I'm concerned, Gorgonzola does the job best. Its saltiness works really well with the somewhat bland polenta.

250g (9oz) butternut squash, peeled, deseeded and cut into chunks

1 medium red onion, quartered

4 medium carrots, peeled and halved lengthways

2 large turnips, peeled and cut into wedges

8–12 mild Italian (see p.36) or game sausages (see p.41)

2 tbsp olive oil

4 sprigs of rosemary, coarsely chopped

150g (5½oz) vacuum-packed or defrosted frozen chestnuts

salt and freshly ground black pepper

FOR THE POLENTA

600ml (1 pint) full-fat milk

6 tbsp double cream

175g (6oz) quick-cook polenta

75g (2½oz) Gorgonzola cheese

25g (scant 1oz) unsalted butter

salt and freshly ground black pepper

1 Preheat the oven to 190°C (375°F/Gas 5).

2 Place the squash, onion, carrots and turnips in a roasting tin with the sausages, and drizzle over the oil. Sprinkle with the rosemary and season with salt and pepper to taste. Place in the preheated oven and bake for 15–20 minutes, turning occasionally until golden and cooked through.

3 Add the chestnuts and return to the oven for 10 minutes more, until the sausages and vegetables are cooked and golden.

4 Meanwhile, prepare the polenta. Put the milk and cream in a pan over a medium heat and bring to the boil. Reduce the heat to a simmer and add the polenta in a thin stream. Stir well, then cook for 20 minutes, or until the polenta is soft and smooth, then beat in the Gorgonzola and butter, and season with salt and pepper to taste.

5 To serve, divide the polenta between 4 serving plates, add the sausages, tumble the vegetables on top and serve immediately.

Balsamic-roasted Sicilian sausages

This dish has an unusual combination of ingredients but they work together extremely well. Use the best balsamic vinegar you can: it makes a real difference to the finished result. If you're a purist, you can peel the grapes, but it doesn't matter if you don't. I suggest serving these sausages with roasted new potatoes in their skins and French beans or another green vegetable such as broccoli.

2 tbsp vegetable oil

8–12 Sicilian sausages

1 large butternut squash, peeled, deseeded and cut into large chunks

4 sprigs of rosemary

4 tbsp balsamic vinegar

1 tbsp molasses or clear honey

400ml (14fl oz) chicken stock

25g (scant 1oz) unsalted butter, chilled and cut into small dice

50g (1¾oz) walnut halves

150g (5½oz) seedless green or red grapes

2 tbsp raisins

salt and freshly ground black pepper

1 Preheat the oven to 200°C (400°F/Gas 6).

2 Heat the oil in a roasting tin or flameproof dish on the hob over a medium heat. Add the sausages, squash and rosemary and season with salt and pepper to taste, then toss together well, place in the preheated oven and cook for 20 minutes, stirring occasionally.

3 Add the balsamic vinegar, then roll the sausages in the mixture to coat them with the glaze. Return to the oven and cook for 10 minutes more. Remove the sausages with a slotted spoon and set aside.

4 Return the roasting tin to the hob. Over a low heat, add the molasses or honey and the stock. Stir gently, then whisk in the chilled butter.

5 Add the walnuts, grapes and raisins and continue cooking over a low heat for 5 minutes, then return the sausages to the tin and stir to coat them with the sauce.

6 Return the roasting tin to the oven and cook for 5 minutes more. Serve immediately.

Pancetta-roasted Italian sausages
with fennel and olive gremolata

Gremolata, or gremolada, is a herb condiment that is often used in Italian cooking with meats, fish and vegetables. It is made by mixing garlic, lemon zest and coarsely chopped parsley. Nowadays chefs play with other combinations, for example using mint to replace the parsley. In this instance I have added some chopped black olives.

2 medium heads of fennel or baby fennel, trimmed and cut into wedges

25g (scant 1oz) unsalted butter

2 tsp caster sugar

2 tbsp balsamic vinegar

100ml (3½fl oz) red wine

8 mild Italian sausages (see p.36), halved

8 thin slices of unsmoked pancetta, halved

2 tbsp olive oil

650ml (23fl oz) chicken stock

250g (9oz) gnocchi

100g (3½oz) sunblush tomatoes in oil, drained

FOR THE GREMOLATA

1 garlic clove, finely chopped

2 tbsp coarsely chopped flat-leaf parsley

grated zest of ½ lemon

8 black olives, pitted and finely chopped

salt and freshly ground black pepper

1 Preheat the oven to 180°C (350°F/Gas 4).

2 Blanch the fennel in a pan of boiling water for 2 minutes. Drain and dry on a clean tea towel.

3 Heat a frying pan over a medium heat then add the butter and fennel. Sprinkle over the sugar, mix well and cook for 5 minutes, stirring occasionally until lightly caramelised.

4 Add the balsamic vinegar and red wine and cook for 2 minutes more. Transfer the fennel and its juices to a roasting tin.

5 Wrap each sausage half in half a slice of pancetta then place on top of the fennel.

6 Drizzle over the oil, pour over the chicken stock and place in the preheated oven for 25 minutes. Baste frequently with the cooking juices.

7 Meanwhile, cook the gnocchi in a pan of lightly salted water following the packet instructions. Drain well.

8 Add the gnocchi to the roasting tin together with the tomatoes, and cook for 5 minutes more.

9 Meanwhile, make the gremolata. Put all the ingredients in a bowl, mix together well and season with salt and pepper to taste.

10 Add the gremolata to the roasting tin and toss everything together. Serve immediately.

Cajun andouille and spoon bread bake

This dish might well be dubbed the American version of the great British toad-in-the-hole. Instead of topping the sausages with the classic batter, you use a cornmeal batter to make a sort of spoon bread soufflé. Spoon bread comes from the American Southern States. For an extra treat, you could top the bake with some sautéed wild mushrooms, cooked in a little butter with chopped chives.

2 tbsp vegetable oil

450g (1lb) cajun andouille sausage (see p.33)

1 small red pepper, halved, deseeded and cut into 1cm (½in) dice

1 yellow pepper, halved, deseeded and cut into 1cm (½in) dice

100g (3½oz) tinned sweetcorn, drained and rinsed

150g (5½oz) ground cornmeal

50g (1¾oz) unsalted butter

2 large eggs

200ml (7fl oz) full-fat milk

4 tsp baking powder

1 tsp caster sugar

100g (3½oz) Cheddar cheese, finely grated

salt and freshly ground black pepper

1 Preheat the oven to 180°C (350°F/Gas 4).

2 Heat the oil in a large frying pan then add the sausages and peppers and cook over a medium heat for 15 minutes, turning regularly until golden and cooked through. Remove with a slotted spoon and leave to cool.

3 When cool enough to handle, cut into 2.5cm (1in) thick slices and place in the bottom of a 25cm (10in) gratin or ovenproof dish with the peppers.

4 Place the sweetcorn kernels and 200ml (7fl oz) of boiling water in a blender, blitz to a smooth liquid, then transfer to a pan and bring to the boil.

5 Reduce the heat, then slowly add the cornmeal, whisking continuously to make a smooth paste. Cook over a gentle heat for 5 minutes.

6 Meanwhile, melt the butter in a small pan over a gentle heat, then stir into the sweetcorn and cornmeal mixture.

7 In a bowl, whisk the eggs until pale and thickened, add the milk, then add to the sweetcorn and cornmeal mixture together with the baking powder. Whisk together well, add the sugar, and season with salt and pepper to taste. Pour the mixture over the sausages.

8 Bake for 20 minutes in the preheated oven, then remove, sprinkle over the cheese and return to the oven for 5 minutes more, until the bake is golden and puffed. Serve immediately.

Sicilian sausage and white bean casserole

Sausages and pulses together are a great match. I particularly love using white beans or lentils. The sage crumb topping gives this dish a wonderful texture.

2 tbsp olive oil

8–12 Sicilian sausages (see p.36)

1 medium onion, finely chopped

4 carrots, peeled and diced

4 sticks celery, trimmed and diced

1 garlic clove, crushed

300ml (½ pint) dry white wine

400ml (14fl oz) passata

600ml (1 pint) chicken stock

2 x 400g (14oz) tins cannellini beans, rinsed and drained

FOR THE SAGE CRUMBS

50g (1¾oz) salted butter

1 garlic clove, crushed

2 tbsp coarsely chopped sage leaves

75g (2½oz) fresh white breadcrumbs

1 Preheat the oven to 180°C (350°F/Gas 4).

2 Heat the oil in a flameproof casserole over a medium heat. Add the sausages and fry for 5 minutes, turning occasionally until golden. Remove with a slotted spoon and set aside.

3 Add the onion, carrots, celery and garlic to the casserole and cook for 4–5 minutes, turning regularly until they begin to soften. Add the wine, increase the heat, and boil for 2 minutes.

4 Add the passata, stock and beans, bring to the boil again, then return the sausages to the casserole and reduce the heat to a simmer. Cover, then put in the preheated oven for 20 minutes.

5 Meanwhile, make the sage crumbs. Melt the butter in a pan over a medium heat. When the butter begins to foam, add the garlic, sage and breadcrumbs. Cook for 2 minutes, until golden and crispy.

6 Sprinkle the sage crumbs over the top of the casserole and return to the oven for 5 minutes more, or until the crust is golden and bubbling. Allow to cool slightly before serving.

Caerphilly rarebit tart

It's important to use a fairly mild-flavoured cheese for this dish as a mature cheese will overpower the sausages. And there's no need to worry about making your own puff pastry or red onion marmalade if you don't want to. You can easily buy excellent ready-rolled puff pastry. Just make sure you choose one of the more expensive ones as it's likely to be made from better-quality butter. Red onion marmalade or relish is available from good stores and delis. Serve with some buttered green beans and mint-flavoured new potatoes.

375g (13oz) ready-rolled puff pastry

plain flour, for dusting

8–12 pork and leek sausages (see p.30)

2 tbsp olive oil

1 free-range egg beaten with 1 tbsp full-fat milk

100g (3½oz) red onion marmalade

1 tsp coarsely chopped thyme leaves

FOR THE RAREBIT

100ml (3½fl oz) whipping cream

75ml (3fl oz) pale ale

1 tsp plain flour

75g (2½oz) Caerphilly or other mild cheese, finely grated

dash of Worcestershire sauce

1 free-range egg yolk

1 tsp Dijon mustard

1 Preheat the oven to 200°C (400°F/Gas 6).

2 Roll the puff pastry out on a floured board to about 23cm x 23cm (9in x 9in). Place on a baking sheet and refrigerate until ready for use.

3 Meanwhile, put the sausages in a roasting tin, drizzle over a little oil and cook in the preheated oven for 10 minutes, or until cooked through. Remove from the oven and leave to cool slightly, then remove the sausages from the tin with a slotted spoon and cut into diagonal 1cm (½in) slices.

4 Remove the pastry from the fridge and brush a 1cm (½in) border of beaten egg and milk around the edge.

5 Place the onion marmalade in the centre of the pastry and spread it all over, leaving the border clear.

6 Sprinkle over the thyme leaves, then add rows of overlapping sausage slices, again leaving the border clear.

7 Place in the preheated oven and bake for 15–20 minutes, or until slightly crisp around the edges.

8 Meanwhile, make the rarebit. Put the cream and ale in a pan over a medium heat. Bring to the boil, then whisk in the flour, cheese and Worcestershire sauce. Reduce the heat and cook, stirring constantly until smooth, about 30 seconds. Remove from the heat, cool slightly, then beat in the egg yolk and mustard.

9 Spoon a little of the rarebit carefully over the sausage tart, then return to the oven for 2–3 minutes, until golden and bubbling. Allow to cool slightly before serving.

Smoky paprika-baked sausages
with patatas bravas

Here is a taste of Spain conjured out of a single baking tin. Patatas bravas – literally 'fierce potatoes' – are crisply fried or roasted potatoes tossed in a piquant tomato sauce. The combination is delicious. In this recipe I've marinated the sausages in a smoky glaze for even more great flavour. Grilled baby courgettes are a nice accompaniment.

2 tbsp olive oil

1 garlic clove, crushed

1 tsp finely chopped thyme leaves

1 tsp smoked Spanish paprika

1 tbsp sherry vinegar

8–12 Lincolnshire sausages (see p.30)

salt and freshly ground black pepper

FOR THE POTATOES

6 tbsp olive oil

2 garlic cloves, crushed

1 tsp dried red chilli flakes

1 tsp smoked Spanish paprika

½ tsp cumin seeds

75ml (3fl oz) sherry vinegar

2 x 400g (14oz) tins peeled and chopped plum tomatoes, with juice

2 tbsp caster sugar

1 bay leaf

1 tsp finely chopped thyme leaves

1 tsp finely chopped fresh oregano or ½ tsp dried oregano

400g (14oz) large floury potatoes (such as Maris Piper or Desirée)

2 tbsp coarsely chopped coriander leaves

salt and freshly ground black pepper

1 The day before, put the oil, garlic, thyme, smoked paprika, vinegar, salt and pepper in a bowl. Whisk together, then pour over the sausages in a bowl. Cover with clingfilm and leave overnight to marinate.

2 The next day, preheat the oven to 200°C (400°F/Gas 6).

3 Prepare the potatoes. Heat a frying pan over a medium heat, then add 2 tbsp of the oil, the garlic and the chilli flakes, and cook, stirring occasionally until softened, for about 1 minute.

4 Add the smoked paprika, cumin seeds and vinegar and cook for 1 minute more, then add the tomatoes and their juice and bring to the boil.

5 Add the sugar, bay leaf, thyme and oregano. Reduce the heat and simmer gently for 10–12 minutes, or until the tomatoes thicken and half the juice has evaporated.

6 Meanwhile, peel the potatoes and cut into fairly large chunks. Put in a pan of lightly salted water, bring to the boil, reduce the heat and parboil for 2 minutes. Drain, then dry in a clean tea towel.

7 Place the remaining olive oil in a roasting tin, toss with the potatoes, and season lightly with salt and pepper.

8 Add the marinated sausages, then bake in the preheated oven for 15–20 minutes, or until the sausages are cooked and the potatoes are golden. Add the tomato sauce and mix together well.

9 Return to the oven for 5 minutes more, then stir in the coriander leaves and serve immediately.

Foil-baked pork sausages
with oriental ginger dressing

This dish just oozes aromatic scents and flavours and when you unwrap the foil in front of your guests, they are sure to be impressed. The oriental aromas will pervade the whole room. Freshly steamed jasmine rice or egg noodles make the perfect accompaniment.

8–10 country pork sausages (see p.30)

8 spring onions, trimmed and cut into 2.5cm (1in) lengths

275g (9½oz) Chinese broccoli, trimmed

2 baby bok choy, leaves separated

FOR THE ORIENTAL DRESSING

2.5cm (1in) piece of root ginger, peeled and finely grated

1 garlic clove, crushed

1 green chilli, deseeded and finely chopped

2 tbsp sweet chilli sauce

2 tsp light soy sauce

1 tsp Thai fish sauce (nam pla)

2 tbsp coarsely chopped coriander leaves

1 tbsp rice wine (mirin)

juice of ½ lime

1 Preheat the oven to 200°C (400°F/Gas 6).

2 For the dressing, mix all the ingredients together in a small bowl. Set aside.

3 Place the sausages in a pan of cold water, bring to the boil, reduce the heat to a simmer and cook for 5 minutes. Remove with a slotted spoon, drain well and dry on a clean tea towel. Cut each sausage diagonally in half lengthways and set aside.

4 Put the spring onions, broccoli and bok choy in a pan of boiling salted water and blanch for 2 minutes. Set aside.

5 Tear off 2 sheets of tinfoil, each 20cm x 20cm (8in x 8in). Lay one on top of the other to give double thickness.

6 Place the sausages in the centre of the tinfoil, scatter over the blanched vegetables, then gather up the tinfoil around the sausages. Pour over the dressing, then fold over the top of the tinfoil to seal in all the ingredients.

7 Place in the preheated oven and bake for 15 minutes.

8 To serve, place the foil package on a serving dish on the table and open up the tinfoil in front of your diners.

Bobotie

This recipe comes from the Cape Malay community in South Africa. It is generally made using minced beef delicately flavoured with sweet spices. Here I replace the beef with crumbled South African Boerewors sausage. I think it works extremely well.

2 tbsp vegetable oil

1 medium onion, thinly sliced

1 garlic clove, crushed

625g (1lb 6oz) Boerewors sausages (see p.40), skin removed

2 tsp curry powder

¼ tsp ground cloves

¼ tsp turmeric

generous pinch of ground allspice

2 tbsp mango chutney

50g (1¾oz) raisins

1 tsp caster sugar

FOR THE TOPPING

100ml (3½fl oz) double cream

75ml (3fl oz) full-fat milk

2 free-range eggs

50g (1¾oz) fresh white breadcrumbs

2 tbsp coarsely chopped coriander leaves

1 Preheat the oven to 180°C (350°F/Gas 4).

2 Heat the oil in a large non-stick pan over a medium heat. Add the onion and garlic, and cook for 6–8 minutes, turning occasionally until the onions are light gold in colour.

3 Add the sausages and cook for 5 minutes, stirring occasionally and breaking the sausage up with a fork as it cooks, then add the curry powder, cloves, turmeric, allspice, chutney, raisins and sugar. Cook for 5 minutes more, stirring occasionally, then transfer to a small ovenproof dish and set aside.

4 For the topping, mix all the ingredients together in a bowl.

5 Pour the topping over the sausage mixture, then place in the preheated oven and bake for 10–15 minutes, or until the topping has set. Leave to cool slightly before serving.

Mustard-glazed Italian sausages
with cipolline 'agrodolce'

Literally translated, 'agrodolce' means sweet and sour and that's the flavour combination achieved in this onion and fig relish. It is delicious served cold as a condiment for cured meats or ham but here I use it warm to accompany the sausages. I recommend you make the agrodolce a few days in advance so the flavours can develop. Both polenta and risotto are a good accompaniment to these sausages.

8–12 hot Italian (see p.36) or
Cumberland sausages (see p.31)
2 tbsp olive oil
1 tbsp Dijon mustard

FOR THE AGRODOLCE
450g (1lb) cipolline or button onions
100g (3½oz) caster sugar
100ml (3½fl oz) red wine
300g (11oz) dried figs
75g (2½oz) currants
100ml (3½fl oz) red wine vinegar
2 tbsp olive oil
1 bay leaf
1 tbsp balsamic vinegar
salt and freshly ground black pepper

1 Prepare the agrodolce a day or two in advance. Blanch the onions in a pan of boiling water over a high heat for 1 minute. Remove with a slotted spoon into a bowl of cold water, then peel and set aside.

2 Put the sugar and 200ml (7fl oz) of water in another pan over a gentle heat, slowly bring to the boil, then increase the heat and cook until the syrup turns golden.

3 Remove from the heat and add the wine. The syrup will harden or caramelise.

4 Return the pan to a low heat and simmer until the caramel dissolves, then add the figs, currants, onions, red wine vinegar, oil, a little salt and pepper and the bay leaf. Simmer until the onions are tender, about 20–25 minutes.

5 Remove the onions to a bowl with a slotted spoon and set aside, then increase the heat under the pan, bring the liquid to the boil, and boil for 10 minutes, or until the liquid is reduced to half its volume.

6 Add the balsamic vinegar, then return the onions to the mix. Cool to room temperature, then chill until ready for use.

7 When you are ready to make the complete dish, preheat the oven to 190°C (375°F/Gas 5).

8 Place the sausages in a roasting tin, pour over the olive oil and place in the preheated oven. Cook for 15–20 minutes, turning occasionally until the sausages are golden.

9 Brush the sausages liberally with the Dijon mustard and return to the oven for 10 minutes more.

10 To serve, carefully reheat the agrodolce in a small pan over a medium heat. Serve alongside the sausages.

The Big Apple Italian pizza

Some of the best pizzas I've tasted outside Italy have been in New York. Here is one of my favourites, made simply with hot Italian sausage, oregano, ricotta and plump olives. In New York they generally like their pizzas with a thin crust so they can pick it up and fold it, so make sure you roll your base out thinly.

FOR THE BASE

2 tsp dried yeast

450g (1lb) strong white bread flour, plus extra for dusting

1 tsp salt

2 tbsp olive oil, plus extra for oiling

FOR THE TOPPING

2 tbsp vegetable oil

4 hot Italian sausages (see p.36)

125g (4½oz) firm ricotta cheese

2 tsp chopped oregano leaves

25g (scant 1oz) pitted black olives, coarsely chopped

2 firm, ripe plum tomatoes, peeled and coarsely chopped

50g (1¾oz) provolone cheese, coarsely grated

olive oil, for drizzling

50g (1¾oz) small rocket leaves, to garnish

1 For the base, measure out 300ml (½ pint) of tepid water. Dissolve the yeast in a little of the water. Sift the flour and salt into a bowl, make a well in the centre and pour in the yeast liquid, together with the oil and the remaining water.

2 Bring the ingredients together with your hands to form pliable dough, then knead on a lightly floured surface for 5–6 minutes, until smooth and elastic.

3 Place in a lightly oiled bowl, cover with a damp cloth, and leave at room temperature for 1 hour, or until doubled in size.

4 For the topping, preheat the oven to 200°C (400°F/Gas 6) and line 2 baking sheets with parchment paper.

5 Heat the vegetable oil in a frying pan over a medium heat. Add the sausages and cook for 15 minutes, turning regularly until golden and cooked through. Remove with a slotted spoon and leave to cool. When cool enough to handle, cut into 1cm (½in) thick slices.

6 Remove the dough from the bowl, divide into 4 pieces, then roll each piece out into a 20cm (8in) rough circle or oval. Place 2 circles on each baking sheet.

7 Mix the ricotta and oregano together in a bowl, then spread over each pizza base. Scatter over the sausage slices, olives and tomatoes, then sprinkle with the provolone and drizzle over a little olive oil.

8 Bake in the preheated oven for 15–20 minutes, or until golden and crispy. Serve immediately, sprinkled with rocket leaves.

Sausage parmigiano

One of our guests at The Lanesborough simply adores the classic aubergine parmigiano. I make it for him regularly when he's staying with us. One day I added some luganega sausage to it by way of a change and it went down a storm, so here's the recipe. Serve it on its own or with a mixed salad dressed with balsamic vinaigrette.

8 tbsp olive oil

1 medium onion, coarsely chopped

2 garlic cloves, crushed

450g (1lb) luganega sausage, skin removed

400g (14oz) tin peeled and chopped plum tomatoes

2 tbsp tomato purée

1 tsp coarsely chopped oregano

1 tbsp coarsely chopped basil leaves

2 large aubergines, cut into 1cm (½in) slices

unsalted butter, for greasing

2 x 125g (4½oz) buffalo mozzarella, thickly sliced

2 tbsp finely grated Parmesan

salt and freshly ground black pepper

1 Preheat the oven to 180°C (350°F/Gas 4).

2 Heat 2 tbsp of the oil in a pan over a medium heat. Add the onion, garlic and sausage and cook for 5–6 minutes, stirring occasionally until the onion has softened. Break the sausage up with a fork as it cooks.

3 Add the tomatoes, tomato purée, oregano and basil, increase the heat and bring to the boil.

4 Reduce the heat and simmer for 15–20 minutes, or until the sauce is thick and pulpy. Season with salt and pepper to taste.

5 Meanwhile, heat the remaining oil in a high-sided frying pan over a medium heat. Add some of the aubergine slices and fry, turning regularly until golden. Remove with a slotted spoon onto kitchen paper to drain. Repeat with the remaining aubergine slices. Season with salt and pepper to taste.

6 Lightly grease a 23cm x 23cm (9in x 9in) ovenproof baking dish, then spoon in some of the sausage and tomato sauce and add a layer of fried aubergine. Repeat, alternating sauce and aubergine, until both have been used up.

7 Arrange the mozzarella slices on top, sprinkle over the Parmesan and place in the preheated oven for 20–25 minutes, or until the top is golden and bubbling. Allow to cool slightly before serving.

Sausage, portobello mushroom
and winter root 'soufflette'

This dish is based on a traditional cottage pie but instead of mashed potato, I use parsnip and swede – two of my favourite root vegetables – to make a deliciously light and airy soufflé-style topping. Beneath the topping lies a rich red-wine-braised sausage mix with mushrooms and shallots. Serve with buttered cabbage and enjoy!

2 tbsp olive oil

200g (7oz) dry-cure back bacon, cut into small dice

10 Cumberland (see p.31) or Lincolnshire sausages (see p.30), each cut into 4

300g (11oz) shallots

400g (14oz) carrots, peeled and cut into 1cm (½in) slices

1 tsp caster sugar

2 tbsp plain flour

300ml (½ pint) red wine

1 tsp finely chopped thyme leaves

100ml (3½fl oz) Madeira (preferably sweet)

600ml (1 pint) beef stock

200g (7oz) small portobello mushrooms, cut into 1cm (½in) slices

FOR THE TOPPING

450g (1lb) swedes

450g (1lb) parsnips

25g (scant 1oz) unsalted butter

25g (scant 1oz) plain flour

100ml (3½fl oz) full-fat milk

2 large free-range eggs, separated

75g (2½oz) Cheddar cheese, coarsely grated

salt and freshly ground black pepper

1 Preheat the oven to 190°C (375°F/Gas 5).

2 Heat the oil in a non-stick frying pan over a medium heat. Add the bacon and sausage pieces and fry for 1–2 minutes, turning occasionally until golden. Remove to a plate with a slotted spoon and set aside.

3 Soak the shallots in very hot water for 5 minutes, then peel and cut in half.

4 Add the shallots and carrots to the pan and fry, turning regularly until golden, about 2–3 minutes, then sprinkle over the sugar and cook, stirring, until lightly caramelised. Sprinkle over the flour and cook, stirring, for 1 minute more.

5 Add the wine and stir well, then add the thyme, Madeira and beef stock. Reduce the heat and simmer for 15–20 minutes.

6 Add the sliced mushrooms, return the bacon and sausages to the sauce, and simmer for 10 minutes more, until the sauce is thick. Transfer to an ovenproof casserole or gratin dish.

7 Make the topping. Peel the swede and parsnips, remove the woody core from the parsnips, then cut both vegetables into small chunks. Put in a pan of lightly salted water, bring to the boil, reduce the heat and cook for 25–30 minutes, or until the vegetables are very tender.

8 Remove from the heat, drain well, mash thoroughly with a potato masher or potato ricer, then return to the pan over a low heat to dry. Season well with salt and pepper to taste and set aside.

9 Melt the butter in a pan over a low heat and when it is hot, add the flour and cook gently for 1 minute, stirring continuously with a wooden spoon. Gradually add the milk and bring to the boil, stirring all the time. Cook for 2–3 minutes, stirring, until the mixture is smooth and thick.

10 Remove from the heat, add the mashed vegetables, then beat in the egg yolks.

11 Whisk the egg whites in a clean bowl until stiff but not dry, then fold lightly into the mixture.

12 Spread the soufflé mixture over the sausages and sprinkle with the cheese.

13 Transfer to the preheated oven and bake for 20–25 minutes, until the topping is risen and golden. Serve immediately.

Madeira-glazed sausages with
parsnip purée, sautéed sprouts and plum relish

Each winter I eagerly await the arrival of Brussels sprouts in the shops. Unlike many folk, I love Brussels sprouts, especially when they're sautéed with a little bacon and are a bit on the crunchy side. If you make the plum relish a few days in advance, the flavour has a chance to develop.

8 pork and apple sausages (see p.30)

2 tbsp olive oil

100ml (3½fl oz) Madeira

4 sage leaves, finely chopped

400ml (14fl oz) chicken stock

FOR THE PARSNIP PURÉE

6 large parsnips

275ml (9fl oz) full-fat milk

200ml (7fl oz) double cream

salt and freshly ground black pepper

FOR THE SPROUTS

425g (15oz) Brussels sprouts

25g (scant 1oz) unsalted butter

2 garlic cloves, peeled and bruised

100g (3½oz) pancetta, finely chopped

salt and freshly ground black pepper

FOR THE PLUM RELISH

25g (scant 1oz) unsalted butter

1 medium red onion, thinly sliced

4 plums, pitted and cut into
2.5cm (1in) dice

20g (¾oz) raisins

2 tbsp honey

1 tbsp balsamic vinegar

pinch of cumin

salt and freshly ground black pepper

1 Prepare the relish a day or two in advance. Heat the butter in a small pan over a medium heat. Add the onion and cook, stirring occasionally for 10 minutes, until softened and lightly caramelised. Add the remaining ingredients and 125ml (4fl oz) of water, then cook gently until the plums are soft and sticky and the liquid has nearly all evaporated. Season with salt and pepper to taste. Transfer to a lidded container and keep covered in the fridge until ready for use.

2 When you are ready to make the complete dish, preheat the oven to 200°C (400°F/Gas 6).

3 For the parsnip purée, peel the parsnips, remove the woody core, then cut into chunks. Place in a pan and add the milk and cream. Bring to the boil, then reduce the heat and simmer for 20 minutes, or until the parsnips are tender.

4 Drain well, transfer to a blender and blitz to a smooth purée. Place in a clean pan, reheat over a medium heat until warm, then season with salt and pepper to taste. Remove from the heat and cover the pan to keep warm.

5 Meanwhile, place the sausages in a roasting tin, brush with the olive oil and place in the preheated oven. Cook for 10 minutes, until golden, then add the Madeira, sage and stock, and return to the oven for 10 minutes more.

6 Meanwhile prepare the sprouts by trimming and scoring the root end. Put in a pan of boiling salted water and simmer for 10–12 minutes, or until just tender. Drain, leave to cool, then cut into halves. Set aside.

7 In a frying pan, heat the butter over a medium heat, add the garlic and pancetta, and cook for 5 minutes, stirring occasionally until golden.

8 Add the sprouts, sauté for 2 minutes, stirring occasionally, then remove the garlic from the pan. Season with salt and pepper to taste.

9 Place the sausages on serving plates, pile on the parsnip purée and put the sprouts alongside. Pour over the pan juices from the sausages and serve immediately with the relish on the side.

Toad-in-the-hole

Consisting of sausages set in a golden pillow of crispy batter, old-fashioned toad-in-the-hole is one of the great British classics. Just like sausages and mash, it has never fallen from favour. Traditionally it was created as a way of using up leftover meat, but over the years the meat was replaced by the great British banger. It is one of the easiest dishes to prepare and is delicious served with gravy. You could try the sage and onion gravy on page 108. Note that this recipe serves six people.

2 tbsp olive oil

18 Lincolnshire (see p.30) or Cumberland sausages (see p.31), or other plump pork sausages of your choice

FOR THE BATTER

300ml (½ pint) full-fat milk

4 free-range eggs

250g (9oz) plain flour, sifted

salt and freshly ground black pepper

1 Preheat the oven to 200°C (400°F/Gas 6).

2 To make the batter, put the milk, eggs and salt and pepper in a large bowl and beat together well. Stir the flour in gradually with a wooden spoon until smooth, then leave to rest for 15 minutes.

3 Divide the oil between two large 6-cup muffin tins and place in the preheated oven until the oil starts to smoke. Cut the sausages in half and place 3 halves in each muffin cup. Roast for 8–10 minutes, turning occasionally until the sausages are browned.

4 Remove from the oven, pour the batter on top of the sausages and return to the oven. Cook for 25 minutes, or until the batter has risen and is crisp and golden brown. Serve with sage and onion gravy (see p.108).

BATTER VARIATIONS

1 Add 1 tsp of finely chopped thyme leaves and 1 tsp of finely chopped sage leaves to the basic batter.

2 Add 1 tbsp of grated horseradish to the batter.

3 Replace half the milk with the same quantity of pale ale.

Wild boar sausages with fennel-braised
potatoes and tomato chermoula

This is a tasty one-pot recipe. The potatoes are braised in the oven, then finished with the sausages, which add even more flavour. Chermoula is a Moroccan condiment. Here I use it as a dressing.

50g (1¾oz) unsalted butter, plus a little for greasing

625g (1lb 6oz) large floury potatoes (such as Maris Piper or Desirée)

1 head of fennel, trimmed and thinly sliced

1 large onion, thinly sliced

750ml (1¼ pints) hot chicken stock

8–12 wild boar sausages

1 tbsp olive oil

salt and freshly ground black pepper

FOR THE CHERMOULA

2 tbsp coarsely chopped flat-leaf parsley

2 tbsp coarsely chopped coriander leaves

2 garlic cloves, crushed

½ tsp paprika

1 tsp ground cumin

3 tbsp olive oil

juice of ½ lemon

2.5cm (1in) piece of root ginger, peeled and finely grated

2 plum tomatoes, peeled and cut into small dice

salt and freshly ground black pepper

1 Preheat the oven to 200°C (400°F/Gas 6) and grease a shallow ovenproof dish with a little of the butter.

2 Peel the potatoes and slice thinly, then put alternating layers of potato, fennel and onion in the dish. Season each layer well with salt and pepper and finish with a layer of neatly overlapping potatoes.

3 Pour over the hot stock until it is just level with the top of the potatoes, then dot the surface with half the remaining butter. Cover with tinfoil and bake for 40 minutes in the preheated oven.

4 Remove from the oven. Melt the remaining butter in a small pan over a gentle heat and use to brush the surface of the potato in the ovenproof dish.

5 Brush the sausages with the oil, place on top of the potatoes, and return to the oven, uncovered, for 20 minutes more to cook the sausages and colour the potatoes.

6 Meanwhile, mix all the ingredients together for the chermoula and season with salt and pepper to taste.

7 Serve the sausages immediately, topped with the chermoula.

Lincolnshire sausages
with cheese and onion mash

This great midweek meal idea is simple to prepare and cook. Although you could use shop-bought tomato pesto, it's not as good as making your own. The pesto here will make more than you need, but you can keep what's left in a sealed container in the fridge for up to a week to use in salads or tossed with pasta.

8–12 Lincolnshire sausages (see p.30)
2 tbsp olive oil
salt and freshly ground black pepper
basil, to garnish

FOR THE MASH
800g (1¾lb) floury potatoes
(such as Maris Piper or Desirée)
2 tbsp double cream
100g (3½oz) mature Cheddar cheese, coarsely grated
4 spring onions, trimmed and finely chopped
salt and freshly ground black pepper

FOR THE PESTO
150g (5½oz) sunblush tomatoes in oil, drained
15g (½oz) fresh basil leaves
2 garlic cloves, peeled
2 tbsp coarsely grated Parmesan
15g (½oz) pine nuts
1 tsp balsamic vinegar
2 tsp caster sugar
175ml (6fl oz) olive oil
salt and freshly ground black pepper

1 Preheat the oven to 200°C (400°F/Gas 6).

2 For the mash, peel the potatoes and cut into large chunks. Put in a pan of lightly salted water, bring to the boil, reduce the heat and cook for 15–20 minutes, or until tender.

3 Drain, then return to the pan. Add the cream then mash with a potato masher or pass through a potato ricer. Beat in the cheese, add the spring onions, and season with salt and pepper to taste. Cover with a lid to keep warm.

4 Put the sausages in a roasting tin, drizzle with oil, season with salt and pepper to taste and place in the preheated oven for 15–20 minutes, until well browned.

5 For the pesto, place all the ingredients except the oil into a liquidiser or blender. With the machine running, slowly add the oil in a thin stream. Blend until smooth, then pour into a small bowl and season with salt and pepper to taste.

6 To serve, pile the mash onto 4 plates, place the sausages on top, drizzle over the pesto and serve, garnished with the basil leaves.

Tartiflette

This French dish, originally from the Savoie region, is made from potatoes, cream, smoked bacon and Reblochon, a soft washed-rind cheese. The name tartiflette is thought to come from 'tartifla' – Savoie's word for potato. Sausages are a natural and delicious addition. Together they make a wonderful baked dish. Serve it with a salad.

200ml (7fl oz) full-fat milk

600ml (1 pint) double cream

1 tsp coarsely chopped thyme leaves

1 small bay leaf

800g (1¾lb) waxy new potatoes (such as Charlotte), peeled

2 tbsp olive oil

1 large onion, thinly sliced

300g (11oz) dry-cured smoked streaky bacon, coarsely chopped

8 Toulouse sausages (see p.32)

1 Reblochon cheese, cut into 1cm (½in) slices

1 tbsp finely chopped fresh chives, to garnish

1 Preheat the oven to 200°C (400°F/Gas 6).

2 Put the milk, cream, thyme and bay leaf in a pan over a medium heat and bring to the boil.

3 Meanwhile, cut the potatoes into 1cm (½in) slices. Add to the pan, reduce the heat and simmer gently for 10 minutes, or until the potatoes are just cooked. Drain well, reserving the cooking liquid. Remove the bay leaf and discard. Set aside.

4 Heat the oil over a medium heat in a frying pan. Add the onion and bacon and sauté for 5 minutes, stirring occasionally until lightly golden and softened. Remove with a slotted spoon to a plate and cover with tinfoil to keep warm.

5 Add the sausages to the pan and fry for 3–4 minutes, stirring occasionally until golden, then remove with a slotted spoon and put in an ovenproof casserole.

6 Add a layer of potatoes on top of the sausages, half the onion and bacon mix, and half the Reblochon cheese. Repeat with another layer of potatoes, followed by the remaining bacon and onion, and top with the remaining cheese.

7 Pour over the cooking liquid from the potatoes to just under the top layer of cheese, then place in the preheated oven and bake for 12–15 minutes, until golden and bubbling. Sprinkle with chives and serve.

Beef sausage hotpot with
beetroot and horseradish relish

Traditional hotpot is made with pieces of lamb or lamb chops but here I use chunky beef sausages and black pudding instead. My beetroot and horseradish relish is the perfect accompaniment. You might like to add some seasonal vegetables.

800g (1¾lb) floury potatoes
(such as Maris Piper or Desirée)

1 tbsp vegetable oil

450g (1lb) beef sausages (see p.37)

1 medium onion, thinly sliced

150g (5½oz) black pudding, cut into
1cm (½in) dice

300g (11oz) turnips, peeled and cut into
1cm (½in) dice

a few sage leaves

a few sprigs of thyme

600ml (1 pint) beef stock

25g (scant 1oz) unsalted butter, chilled
and cut into small dice

salt and freshly ground black pepper

FOR THE RELISH

1 large cooked beetroot, grated

2 tbsp creamed horseradish

1 First make the relish by mixing the beetroot and horseradish sauce together in a bowl. Chill in the fridge until ready to use.

2 Preheat the oven to 180°C (350°F/Gas 4).

3 Peel the potatoes and slice thinly. Put in a pan of lightly salted water, bring to the boil, reduce the heat and cook for 5–8 minutes, until they begin to soften. Drain and set aside.

4 Heat the oil in a large heavy-based pan over a medium heat. Add the sausages and onion and brown for 6–8 minutes, turning occasionally. Remove the sausages with a slotted spoon, cut in half and set aside.

5 Combine the browned onion with the cooked potato in a bowl, then place a layer of onion and potato in the bottom of an ovenproof casserole dish. Season with salt and pepper to taste.

6 Top with the sausages, half the black pudding, half the turnips and the sage and thyme. Add the remaining black pudding and turnips and pour over the stock. Top with the remaining onion and potato, then dot with butter.

7 Cover with a tight-fitting lid or tinfoil and cook in the preheated oven for 40 minutes. Uncover and cook for 10 minutes more, or until the surface is browned and golden.

8 Serve the hotpot with the beetroot and horseradish relish.

stovetop

Simple sausage cassoulet

This traditional French speciality from Gascony is normally made using cured duck legs preserved in salt, thyme and garlic. My recipe uses two types of sausage instead – Toulouse sausages and saucisse de morteau – but it's just as tasty. If you can't find saucisse de morteau, any other quality cured and smoked pork sausage would be good.

2 tbsp olive oil

8 Toulouse sausages (see p.32), each cut into 4 pieces

200g (7oz) saucisse de morteau, cut into 1cm (½in) dice

50g (1¾oz) belly of pork, cut into lardons

300ml (½ pint) dry white wine

300g (11oz) haricot beans, soaked overnight in cold water and drained

2 medium onions, coarsely chopped

1 tsp finely chopped thyme leaves

2 small bay leaves

4 large garlic cloves, crushed

400g (14oz) tin peeled and chopped plum tomatoes

1 litre (1¾ pints) chicken stock

4 tbsp coarse fresh white breadcrumbs

2 tbsp coarsely chopped flat-leaf parsley

1 Heat the oil in a heavy-based casserole over a medium heat. Add the pieces of Toulouse sausage and fry for 1–2 minutes, turning occasionally until golden, then add the saucisse de morteau and the pork belly lardons, and fry for 5 minutes more, stirring occasionally until golden.

2 Pour over the wine and cook for 10 minutes, or until the wine has reduced by two-thirds, then add the beans, onions, thyme, bay leaves and half the garlic, together with the tomatoes. Stir well.

3 Add the stock and bring to the boil. Reduce the heat, cover the casserole and simmer gently for 3–3½ hours, until the beans are cooked but still have some bite. Alternatively, put the casserole in a preheated oven at 180°C (350°F/ Gas 4) for 3–3½ hours.

4 Meanwhile, mix the remaining garlic with the breadcrumbs and parsley. Preheat the grill.

5 Sprinkle the breadcrumb mix evenly over the top of the casserole and place under the hot grill until the sauce bubbles and the breadcrumbs are golden. Serve immediately.

Pork and black bean chilli verde

You can make this dish as hot as you like. It all depends on your taste. The more green chillies you add, the hotter it will be.

1 tbsp vegetable oil

400g (14oz) pork and chilli sausages (see p.30), each cut into 4 pieces

1 medium onion, finely chopped

2 garlic cloves, crushed

400g (14oz) cooked turtle beans

600ml (1 pint) chicken stock

tortilla chips, to serve

sour cream, to serve

FOR THE CHILLI VERDE

4 green tomatoes, coarsely chopped

2 small green chillies, finely chopped

2 green peppers, halved, deseeded and coarsely chopped

3 tbsp coarsely chopped coriander leaves

1 tbsp ground cumin

1 tbsp caster sugar

4 spring onions, trimmed and coarsely chopped

100g (3½oz) spinach leaves

1 For the chilli verde, place all the ingredients in a blender and blitz until coarse in texture. Remove to a bowl and set aside.

2 Heat a high-sided frying pan over a medium heat. When the pan is hot, add the oil then the pieces of sausage. Fry for 4 minutes, stirring occasionally until golden.

3 Add the onion and garlic and cook for 5–6 minutes more, stirring occasionally until the onion is softened. Add the beans, stock and chilli verde, mix well, then cover the pan.

4 Reduce the heat and simmer gently, stirring occasionally for 20 minutes, until the sauce has thickened.

5 Transfer to serving bowls and serve immediately with the tortilla chips and sour cream.

Hunter-style Italian sausages

Serve these braised sausages at their simplest over some olive-oil mash potatoes or Parmesan-flavoured polenta. I promise you, you won't be disappointed.

2 tbsp olive oil

450g (1lb) Luganega or mild Italian sausages (see p.36), cut into approx. 10cm (4in) lengths

pinch of dried red chilli flakes

2 garlic cloves, crushed

2 red peppers, halved, deseeded and cut into strips

100ml (3½fl oz) dry white wine

400g (14oz) tin peeled plum tomatoes

1 tbsp tomato purée

1 tsp caster sugar

50g (1¾oz) pitted black olives

1 tsp coarsely chopped oregano leaves

10 basil leaves, plus extra leaves to garnish

salt and freshly ground black pepper

1 Heat the oil in a large frying pan over a medium heat. Add the sausages and fry for 5 minutes, turning occasionally until golden, then add the chilli, garlic, peppers and a pinch of salt, and cook for 5 minutes.

2 Add the white wine, cover the pan and cook for 2 minutes, then add the tomatoes, tomato purée and sugar. Increase the heat and bring to the boil.

3 Add the olives, oregano and basil, cover the pan again, and reduce the heat. Simmer for 10–15 minutes, stirring occasionally until the sausages are cooked through and the sauce has thickened.

4 Adjust the seasoning, garnish with some more basil leaves and serve immediately.

Toulouse sausages with lentils,
sweet tomatoes and smoked bacon

Sausages and lentils are a marriage made in heaven. Here they combine to make a dish that's really earthy. I love it! Toulouse sausages are the perfect variety to use, but I enjoy it with Cumberland sausages too. Serve with a creamy potato and leek mash.

2 tbsp olive oil

8–12 Toulouse sausages (see p.32)

250g (9oz) smoked bacon, cut into 1cm (½in) dice

1 medium onion, finely chopped

1 carrot, peeled and cut into small dice

150g (5½oz) sunblush tomatoes in oil, drained

1 tbsp clear honey

350g (12oz) Puy lentils

1 litre (1¾ pints) chicken stock

1 small bay leaf

1 small sprig of thyme

salt and freshly ground black pepper

2 tbsp coarsely chopped flat-leaf parsley, to serve

1 Heat the oil in a heavy-based flameproof casserole over a medium heat. Reduce the heat, then add the sausages and fry for 5 minutes, turning occasionally until golden. Remove with a slotted spoon and set aside.

2 Add the bacon to the casserole and fry for 7–8 minutes, stirring occasionally until golden, then add the onion and carrot, stir and cook for 2–3 minutes, until softened.

3 Add the tomatoes and honey and cook for 2 minutes more, then add the lentils, pour over the stock, increase the heat and bring to the boil.

4 Add the bay leaf and thyme, then return the sausages to the casserole, mix well, reduce the heat and simmer for 10–15 minutes, or until the lentils have softened.

5 To serve, season with salt and pepper to taste and stir in the chopped parsley.

Indian sausage masala

Sausages are terrific at absorbing spicy flavours and sauces, as my sausage masala recipe shows to perfection. Pork or lamb sausages both work well. Serve with naan bread or a cinnamon-flavoured rice pilau. You can readily find curry leaves together with all the spices at Asian grocers.

2 tbsp vegetable oil

¼ tsp mustard seeds

3–4 fresh curry leaves

1cm (½in) piece of root ginger, peeled and finely chopped

2 medium onions, finely chopped

3 garlic cloves, crushed

1 hot green chilli, finely chopped

½ tsp chilli powder

½ tsp turmeric

1 tsp ground coriander

6 cardamom pods, cracked

¼ tsp garam masala

8–12 lamb (see p.39) or Cumberland sausages (see p.31), each cut into 3 pieces

1 tbsp tomato purée

pinch of salt

4 plum tomatoes, cut into small dice

150ml (¼ pint) natural yoghurt

2 tbsp coarsely chopped mint leaves

1 tbsp coriander leaves, to garnish

1 Heat the oil in a high-sided frying pan over a medium heat. Add the mustard seeds and curry leaves. Fry for 10–15 seconds, until the mustard seeds pop.
2 Add the ginger, onions, garlic and chilli and cook for 4–5 minutes, stirring occasionally until the onions are golden, then add the chilli powder, turmeric, coriander, cardamom and garam masala and sauté for 2–3 minutes.
3 Add the pieces of sausage and cook for 10–15 minutes, stirring occasionally until cooked through.
4 Add the tomato purée and salt, stir well, then add 100ml (3½fl oz) of water and the tomatoes. Reduce the heat and cook for 5 minutes, stirring occasionally until fairly dry.
5 Meanwhile, mix together the yoghurt and mint in a small bowl.
6 Sprinkle the coriander over the sausage masala and serve immediately with the yoghurt and mint alongside.

Game sausages
with Barolo sauce

Any type of game sausage – wild boar, pheasant, venison or wild duck – is great for this dish. They are all suitable and all give a delicious result.

8–12 game sausages (see p.41) each cut into 4 pieces

1 tbsp plain flour

2 tbsp olive oil

20g (¾oz) unsalted butter

225g (8oz) piece of streaky bacon, boneless, rindless and cut into lardons

400g (14oz) button mushrooms, halved

300g (11oz) button onions, peeled

3 tbsp balsamic vinegar

2 tbsp redcurrant jelly

600ml (1 pint) Barolo or other full-bodied red wine

200g (7oz) vacuum-packed or defrosted frozen chestnuts

a few sprigs of thyme

50ml (scant 2fl oz) port wine

salt and freshly ground black pepper

1 Dip the pieces of sausage in the flour and shake off any excess.

2 Heat the oil and half the butter in a flameproof casserole over a medium heat. Add the pieces of sausage and fry for 5 minutes, turning occasionally until golden. Remove with a slotted spoon and set aside.

3 Add the bacon and mushrooms to the pan and fry for 7–8 minutes, stirring occasionally until golden. Remove with a slotted spoon and set aside with the sausages.

4 Add the onions and remaining butter and fry for 10 minutes, stirring occasionally until golden, then pour over the vinegar and add the redcurrant jelly. Cook for 5 minutes, until the onions have caramelised.

5 Pour over the red wine and bring to the boil. Reduce the heat to a simmer, then return the sausages, bacon and mushrooms to the pan.

6 Add the chestnuts, tuck in the thyme and cook gently over a low heat for 10–15 minutes, stirring occasionally until the liquid has reduced to give a rich sauce.

7 Add the port wine, season with salt and pepper to taste and serve immediately.

This is the really comforting way to enjoy sausages if ever there was one. Slow-cooked in a rich onion-and-beer braising sauce, these sausages are absolutely delicious. I often serve them on a bed of crushed new potatoes mixed with freshly chopped flat-leaf parsley.

Beer-braised beef sausages with onions

3 tbsp vegetable oil

8–12 beef and ale sausages (see p.37)

1 medium onion, thinly sliced

1 tbsp tomato purée

2 tbsp plain flour

500ml (17fl oz) brown ale

750ml (1¼ pints) beef stock

1 tbsp caster sugar

1 tsp finely chopped thyme leaves

2 small bread rolls, cut into 2.5cm (1in) slices

1 level tbsp Dijon mustard

salt and freshly ground black pepper

1 Heat 1 tbsp of the oil in a deep-sided frying pan over a medium heat. Add the sausages and cook for 5–6 minutes, turning occasionally until golden. Remove with a slotted spoon and set aside.

2 Add the remaining oil to the pan, then add the onion. Fry for about 5 minutes, stirring occasionally until golden, then add the tomato purée and cook for 1 minute more. Stir in the flour and cook for 1 minute more, then add the ale, reduce the heat and simmer for 5 minutes.

3 Add the stock and stir well, then add the sugar and season with salt and pepper to taste.

4 Add the thyme, return the sausages to the sauce and cook for 12–15 minutes, or until the sausages are cooked through. Preheat the grill.

5 Grill the sliced bread on both sides and spread one side with mustard. Top the sausages with the mustard croûtons and serve immediately.

Tunisian sausage stew
with dates and apricots

This hearty stew is made with two types of sausage. Use traditional lamb sausages together with merguez, which is typical of Tunisia, or indeed all of North Africa. The mixture of the varied spices and the sweet fruity sauce gives a wonderful flavour. Delicious with couscous or a chickpea purée.

4 tbsp vegetable oil

2 medium onions, coarsely chopped

1 garlic clove, crushed

8 lamb sausages (see p.39), each cut into 3 pieces

250g (9oz) merguez sausages (see p.38) or if buying, preferably mini merguez

½ tsp ground ginger

1 tsp ground coriander

pinch of saffron strands

½ tsp ground cinnamon

½ tsp paprika

3 aubergines, cut into 1cm (½in) dice

75g (2½oz) pitted dried dates, halved

125g (4½oz) dried apricots, soaked and cut into thin slices

400g (14oz) tin peeled and chopped plum tomatoes

570ml (18fl oz) tomato juice

1 tbsp honey

750ml (1¼ pints) lamb or chicken stock

1 tbsp coarsely chopped mint leaves

75g (2½oz) blanched whole almonds, toasted until golden, to serve

1 tsp sesame seeds, toasted until golden, to serve

1 Heat half the oil in a high-sided frying pan over a medium heat. Add the onions and garlic and fry for 10 minutes, stirring occasionally until golden. Remove with a slotted spoon and set aside.

2 Add the sausages to the pan and fry for 5 minutes, turning occasionally until golden, then add the ginger, coriander, saffron, cinnamon and paprika, together with the remaining oil and the aubergines. Fry for 4–5 minutes, stirring occasionally until the aubergines have started to soften.

3 Add the dates, apricots, tomatoes, tomato juice, honey, stock and mint. Increase the heat and bring to the boil, then reduce the heat and simmer gently for 20 minutes.

4 Return the onions to the pan and simmer for 15 minutes more, until the aubergines, dates and apricots are soft.

5 To serve, sprinkle with the toasted almonds and sesame seeds.

Cotechino with lentils and pear mostarda

Cotechino is a garlicky sausage from northern Italy. It is traditionally eaten with lentils to bring prosperity and good luck for the new year. Uncooked cotechino is difficult to come by so I've used the cooked version for this dish, which works a treat. Serve with roasted parsnips.

500g (1lb 2oz) cooked cotechino

200g (7oz) Castelluccio or Puy lentils

2 tbsp olive oil

75g (2½oz) smoked pancetta, cut into 1cm (½in) dice

1 small onion, coarsely chopped

1 tbsp coarsely chopped sage leaves

2 garlic cloves, crushed

1 large carrot, peeled and coarsely chopped

1 stick celery, trimmed and coarsely chopped

100ml (3½fl oz) passata

300ml (½ pint) chicken stock

salt and freshly ground black pepper

FOR THE PEAR MOSTARDA

200g (7oz) caster sugar

generous pinch of dried red chilli flakes

2 tsp mustard seeds

4 large ripe pears, peeled, cored and cut into 1cm (½in) dice

1 The day before, make the mostarda. Put the sugar and 200ml (7fl oz) of water in a pan over a gentle heat and cook for 10 minutes, until a syrup has formed.

2 Add the chilli, mustard seeds and pears, and continue to cook gently, stirring occasionally until the syrup is thick and the pears are opaque but not mushy. Leave to cool then refrigerate in an airtight container until ready to use.

3 The next day, soak the cotechino in a bowl of cold water for 1½ hours.

4 Meanwhile, put the lentils in a pan, cover with water and bring to the boil. Reduce the heat and cook for 25–30 minutes, until tender, then drain and set aside.

5 Heat the oil in a frying pan over a medium heat. Add the pancetta, onion, sage and garlic, and fry for 4–5 minutes, stirring occasionally until the onion is soft.

6 Add the carrot and celery and cook for 5 minutes more, then add the lentils, passata and stock, and season with salt and pepper to taste. Reduce the heat and simmer for 20 minutes, until all the liquid has been absorbed. Cover the pan and keep warm over a low heat.

7 Meanwhile, remove the cotechino from the water and pierce with a fork 8–10 times. Place in a pan of cold water, bring to the boil, reduce the heat and simmer for 20 minutes.

8 Drain, remove the skin and cut into large chunks. Serve with the lentils and a spoonful of pear mostarda on the side.

Bratwurst with turnip and apple sauerkraut

The Germans are great sausage-makers and they use their sausages to make wonderfully hearty, robust dishes. This recipe uses sauerkraut, that familiar German favourite. Germans often replace the wine in this recipe with beer, especially when the dish is served during Oktoberfest – the annual beer festival that takes place during October.

3 tbsp vegetable oil

175g (6oz) piece of dry-cure smoked streaky bacon, cut into strips (lardons)

1 large onion, thinly sliced

1 garlic clove, crushed

2 medium turnips, peeled and coarsely grated

100ml (3½fl oz) dry white wine (preferably dry Riesling)

1 tbsp brown sugar

10 juniper berries

1 tsp caraway seeds

1 bay leaf

200ml (7fl oz) apple juice

2 Gala apples, peeled, cored and cut into wedges

450g (1lb) tin sauerkraut, drained, rinsed and dried in a tea towel

8 bratwurst (see p.37) or bockwurst sausages

dill pickle slices, to serve

assorted mustards, to serve

1 Heat 2 tbsp of the oil in a flameproof casserole over a high heat. Add the bacon and fry for 6–8 minutes, until the bacon is crisp and its fat is rendered. Remove with a slotted spoon onto kitchen paper to drain.

2 Add the onion, garlic and turnips to the casserole, reduce the heat and cook for 10–15 minutes, stirring occasionally until the onion is soft and transparent.

3 Increase the heat and add the wine, sugar, juniper berries, caraway seeds and bay leaf. Cook for 5 minutes, then add the apple juice, apple wedges and sauerkraut. Cover, reduce the heat and simmer gently for 10–15 minutes, until the apples are just tender.

4 Meanwhile, heat the remaining oil in a frying pan over a medium heat. Add the sausages and cook for 15–20 minutes, turning occasionally until golden and cooked through.

5 Put the sauerkraut mixture on a serving plate, top with the sausages, scatter over the bacon and serve with the accompaniments.

Frying-pan sausages with orange and parsley

This dish is my version of the classic Italian osso bucco, or braised veal shank. It is one of my favourite winter sausage creations. I love serving it on a bed of fragrant saffron-flavoured rice. You can use lamb or country pork sausages. Both are equally delicious.

8–12 lamb (see p.39) or country pork sausages (see p.30)

1 tbsp plain flour

1 tbsp olive oil

15g (½oz) unsalted butter

1 medium onion, cut into 1cm (½in) dice

3 carrots, peeled and cut into 1cm (½in) dice

2 sticks celery, trimmed and cut into 1cm (½in) dice

2 garlic cloves, crushed

½ tsp dried red chilli flakes

2 tbsp tomato purée

250ml (8fl oz) dry white wine

400ml (14fl oz) chicken stock

200ml (7fl oz) orange juice

50ml (scant 2fl oz) Pernod (optional)

4 plum tomatoes, peeled and coarsely chopped

3 tbsp coarsely chopped flat-leaf parsley

1 garlic clove, crushed

grated zest of ½ orange

salt and freshly ground black pepper

1 Lightly dust the sausages in the flour and shake off any excess.

2 Heat the oil in a high-sided non-stick frying pan over a medium heat. Add the sausages and fry for 5 minutes, stirring occasionally until golden. Remove with a slotted spoon and set aside.

3 Add the butter to the pan and when it is hot, add the onion, carrots, celery, garlic and chilli flakes. Fry for 4–5 minutes, stirring occasionally until the vegetables begin to soften but do not colour.

4 Add the tomato purée and cook for 2–3 minutes more, then pour in the wine, bring to the boil and cook for 2 minutes more. Add the stock, orange juice, Pernod, if using, and chopped tomatoes, and season with salt and pepper to taste.

5 Return the sausages to the pan, cover, reduce the heat and simmer for 10–15 minutes, until the sausages are cooked through.

6 Meanwhile, put the parsley, garlic and orange zest in a bowl and mix together well.

7 Serve the sausages topped with the parsley mix.

Spanish sausage stew
with rosemary and parsley oil

This bean and sausage stew comes from Asturias in north-west Spain. It's a heart-warming dish that's known in Asturias as fabada. If you can't get morcilla (Spanish blood sausage), then simply use another type of black pudding. Like all slow-cooked foods this stew tastes even better the next day.

500g (1lb 2oz) Spanish white beans (fabas) or any white beans, soaked overnight in cold water

2 chorizo picante (see p.32), skin removed and cut into large dice

1 morcilla sausage, cut into 5cm (2in) dice

1 litre (1¾ pints) chicken stock or water

2 tbsp olive oil

200g (7oz) boneless and rindless pancetta, cut into 1cm (½in) slices

1 medium onion, coarsely chopped

generous pinch of saffron strands

2 garlic cloves, crushed

1 tsp paprika

1 bay leaf

FOR THE ROSEMARY AND PARSLEY OIL

2 tbsp coarsely chopped flat-leaf parsley

½ tbsp coarsely chopped rosemary leaves

2 tbsp olive oil

1 garlic clove, crushed

juice of ¼ lemon

salt and freshly ground black pepper

1 Drain the beans and place in a large pan or flameproof casserole. Put the chorizo and morcilla on top, then cover with the stock or water and bring to the boil.

2 Reduce the heat and simmer for 2 hours, checking from time to time in case you need to add more water or stock as the ingredients must always be covered with liquid.

3 When the beans and sausage have been simmering for 2 hours, heat the oil over a medium heat in a frying pan. Add the pancetta and fry for 5 minutes, stirring occasionally until golden. Remove with a slotted spoon and add to the beans and sausage.

4 Add the onion, saffron, garlic and paprika to the frying pan and fry for 2–3 minutes, until the onion and garlic have softened. Remove with a slotted spoon and add to the beans and sausage, together with the bay leaf.

5 Simmer the beans and sausage for 1 hour more, adding more stock or water if necessary, though the finished stew should have a thick consistency.

6 Meanwhile, mix all the ingredients for the rosemary and parsley oil together in a bowl and season with salt and pepper to taste.

7 Drizzle the rosemary and parsley oil over the stew and serve immediately.

sauces and relishes

Tasty accompaniments

A simple fried or grilled sausage can be delicious, but sometimes you just want to pep things up. The following pages are crammed with a selection of tasty, easy-to-prepare sauces, relishes and gravies. On days when you simply don't have time to cook, reach for a storecupboard favourite. I always have French mustard to hand – plain or wholegrain Dijon mustard hit the spot for me – but to accompany smoked sausages I prefer a classic sweet American mustard. Then of course your storecupboard must always include those classic all-time winners – ketchup and brown sauce.

Red-hot creole sauce

YIELD 200ML (7FL OZ)

1 tbsp olive oil

2 shallots, coarsely chopped

1 garlic clove, crushed

25g (scant 1oz) demerara sugar

2 tbsp white wine vinegar

400g (14oz) firm ripe tomatoes, blanched, peeled, deseeded and cut into 1cm (½ in) dice

4 tbsp tomato ketchup

2 tsp creole spices seasoning

1 tbsp hot pepper sauce

½ tsp dried oregano

1 tsp Worcestershire sauce

salt and freshly ground black pepper

Put the oil in a pan over a medium heat. Add the shallots and garlic, and cook for 3–4 minutes, stirring occasionally until soft but not coloured. Add the sugar and vinegar and cook for 2 minutes more. Add the tomatoes, ketchup, creole spices, hot pepper sauce, oregano and Worcestershire sauce. Reduce the heat and simmer for 15–20 minutes, stirring occasionally until the mixture has a thick consistency. Season with salt and pepper to taste, then transfer to a blender and blitz until smooth. Transfer to a bowl and leave to cool. This will keep well in the fridge, covered, for up to 1 week.

Mustard and horseradish sauce

YIELD 150ML (¼ PINT)

5cm (2in) piece of fresh horseradish, peeled and finely grated

1 dill pickle, finely chopped

1 tbsp baby capers, rinsed and drained

1 tbsp prepared English mustard

4 tbsp good-quality mayonnaise

4 tbsp thick sour cream or natural yoghurt

salt and freshly ground black pepper

Put all the ingredients, except the sour cream or yoghurt, in a small blender and blitz until smooth. Transfer to a bowl, add the sour cream or yoghurt, and season with salt and pepper to taste. This will keep well in the fridge, covered, for 2–3 days.

Smoky barbecue sauce

YIELD 175ML (6FL OZ)

4 tbsp hot chilli sauce

2 tbsp apple jelly

2 tbsp balsamic vinegar

½ tsp prepared English mustard

1 tbsp Worcestershire sauce

4 tbsp tomato ketchup

1 tsp smoked paprika (pimentón)

pinch of cayenne pepper

2 tbsp demerara sugar

2 tbsp molasses or treacle

2 tbsp tomato purée

Place all the ingredients in a small pan with 150ml (¼ pint) of water. Bring to the boil over a medium heat, reduce the heat and simmer for 10 minutes, stirring frequently until the mixture has a thick, jam-like consistency. Transfer to a bowl and leave to cool. This will keep well in the fridge, covered, for up to 2 weeks.

Beer ketchup sauce

YIELD 400ML (14FL OZ)

200ml (7fl oz) tomato ketchup

50ml (scant 2fl oz) light ale

100ml (3½fl oz) maple syrup

1 tsp allspice

1 garlic glove, crushed

1 tbsp tomato purée

generous pinch of cayenne pepper

1 tbsp cider vinegar

salt and freshly ground black pepper

Mix all the ingredients except the salt and pepper together in a small pan, cook over a low heat for 5 minutes, stirring occasionally, then season with salt and pepper to taste. Transfer to a bowl and leave to cool. This will keep well in the fridge, covered, for 2–3 weeks.

VARIATIONS

WHISKY KETCHUP SAUCE

Replace the light ale with 50ml (scant 2fl oz) Bourbon whisky.

FRUIT KETCHUP SAUCE

Replace the light ale with a fruit-flavoured ale such as blackberry ale or cherry ale. This is especially good with grilled game or wild boar sausages.

Balsamic honey mustard sauce

YIELD 175ML (6FL OZ)

3 tbsp Dijon mustard

4 tbsp clear honey

2 tsp soy sauce

4 tbsp balsamic vinegar

Place all the ingredients in a small pan, add 100ml (3½fl oz) of water and cook over a low heat for 5 minutes, stirring occasionally. Transfer to a bowl and leave to cool. This sauce will keep well in the fridge, covered, for up to 2 weeks.

Souped-up salsa

YIELD 350ML (12 FL OZ)

2 medium onions, finely chopped

200g (7oz) tomatoes, coarsely chopped

½ tsp salt

4 tbsp tomato ketchup

4 hot red chillies, finely chopped

2 tbsp hot pepper sauce

juice of 1 lime

pinch of cayenne pepper

salt and freshly ground black pepper

6 tbsp coarsely chopped coriander leaves

Combine the onions and tomatoes in a bowl, sprinkle with the salt and leave for 1 hour to draw out the excess water. Squeeze any remaining moisture out between the palms of your hands and place in a blender with all the remaining ingredients except the coriander leaves. Blitz to a coarse purée. Transfer to a pan and slowly bring to the boil. Reduce the heat and simmer for 20–25 minutes, until the mixture reduces and becomes syrupy. Leave to cool, stir in the coriander, then transfer to storage jars. Ideally leave for 2–3 days before eating to allow the flavours to develop. This will keep well in the fridge, covered, for up to 2 weeks.

Sweet and sour Asian ketchup

YIELD 175ML (6FL OZ)

25g (scant 1oz) toasted peanuts

2 garlic cloves, crushed

1 tbsp demerara sugar

5cm (2in) piece of root ginger, peeled and finely grated

1 tbsp soy sauce

1 tbsp sesame oil

4 tbsp tomato ketchup

1 tbsp rice wine vinegar

1 tsp chilli oil

1 tsp prepared English mustard

2 tsp toasted sesame seeds

Put the peanuts, garlic, sugar and ginger in a blender and blitz until smooth. Transfer to a bowl, add the soy sauce, sesame oil, ketchup, vinegar, chilli oil, mustard and sesame seeds, and mix well together. This will keep well in the fridge, covered, for up to 1 week.

Salsa verde

YIELD 300ML (½ PINT)

1 garlic clove, peeled

50g (1¾oz) flat-leaf parsley

4 anchovy fillets in oil, drained

1 tsp Dijon mustard

50g (1¾oz) capers, rinsed

25g (scant 1oz) dill pickle

2 tbsp Cabernet Sauvignon red wine vinegar

125ml (4fl oz) olive oil

Place all the ingredients in a small blender and blitz to make a coarse pulp, taking care not to over-process. Transfer to a bowl. This will keep well in the fridge, covered, for up to 2 days.

White barbecue relish

YIELD 200ML (7FL OZ)

2 medium onions, finely grated

150ml (¼ pint) good-quality mayonnaise

3 tbsp cider or wine vinegar

3 tbsp prepared horseradish sauce

½ tsp cayenne pepper

salt and freshly ground black pepper

Place all the ingredients in a bowl with 50ml (scant 2fl oz) of water and mix together until smooth. Chill well before serving. This will keep well in the fridge, covered, for up to 1 week.

Smoked sausage relish

As the title suggests, this relish is particularly good served with grilled smoked sausages.

YIELD 150ML (¼ PINT)

100ml (3½fl oz) tomato chilli ketchup

1 tbsp hot pepper sauce

2 tbsp finely chopped sweet pickle

Place all the ingredients together in a bowl and mix well. This will keep well in the fridge, covered, for up to 1 week.

Sunblush tomato and hot chilli relish

YIELD 300ML (½ PINT)
200g (7oz) sunblush tomatoes in their oil
2 tsp harissa paste
juice of 1 lemon
4 tsp red wine vinegar
4 tbsp caster sugar
salt and freshly ground black pepper

Place all the ingredients except the salt and pepper in a small blender and blitz until smooth. Season to taste. This will keep well in the fridge, covered, for up to 1 week.

Sweet onion and coriander chutney

YIELD 150ML (¼ PINT)
1 tbsp olive oil
2 large red onions, finely chopped
2 garlic cloves, crushed
75ml (3fl oz) balsamic vinegar
50g (1¾oz) demerara sugar
generous pinch of allspice
pinch of ground ginger
2 tbsp redcurrant jelly
2 tbsp coarsely chopped coriander leaves

Heat the oil in a pan over a medium heat. Add the onions and garlic and cook for 5 minutes, stirring occasionally until softened. Add the vinegar, sugar, 100ml (3½fl oz) of water, and the allspice and ginger. Increase the heat and bring to the boil. Reduce the heat and simmer for 10 minutes, or until the liquid has nearly all evaporated and the onions are caramelised. Add the redcurrant jelly and coriander and cook for 1 minute more. Leave to cool. This will keep well in the fridge, covered, for 2–3 days.

VARIATION

ROASTED GARLIC AND ONION CHUTNEY

Put 8 unpeeled garlic cloves in a roasting tin in an oven preheated to 180°C (350°F/Gas 4) for 10–15 minutes, or until caramelised. Remove from the oven, leave to cool slightly, then pop the cloves out of their skins. Mash to a purée with a fork, then proceed as for the Sweet onion and coriander chutney, replacing the crushed garlic with the garlic purée.

Apple chutney

YIELD 1KG (2¼LB)
1kg (2¼lb) Granny Smith apples
1 large onion, finely chopped
100g (3½oz) raisins
200ml (7fl oz) cider vinegar
100ml (3½fl oz) light ale
250g (9oz) demerara sugar
1 tsp each of ground cinnamon, ground ginger, ground coriander
generous pinch each of allspice and ground cloves

Peel, core and roughly chop the apples. Place with the remaining ingredients in a heavy-based pan over a medium heat. Slowly bring to the boil, stirring occasionally. Reduce the heat and simmer for 45 minutes, stirring occasionally until the liquid has reduced and turned into a thick pulp. Spoon into warm, sterilised jars, cover tightly and allow to cool before storing in a cool dark place. Do not refrigerate. This chutney will keep for 3 months, unsealed. Ideally, use within a month of opening.

VARIATION

SPICED APPLE CHUTNEY

Add 1 tsp of dried red chilli flakes to the apple chutney recipe, then proceed according to the recipe.

Clockwise from the top: apple chutney, sweet onion and coriander chutney, sunblush tomato and hot chilli relish

Cranberry and chilli jelly

YIELD 200ML (7FL OZ)

350g (12oz) prepared cranberry sauce

1 small onion, finely chopped

1 red chilli, deseeded and finely chopped

2 tsp caster sugar

juice of ½ lime

2 tbsp hot red chilli jelly

Put all the ingredients in a small pan over a gentle heat with 100ml (3½fl oz) of water. Stir occasionally until the onions have softened and the chilli jelly has melted, about 8–10 minutes. Transfer to a small blender and blitz until smooth, then put in a bowl and leave to cool. This will keep well in the fridge, covered, for up to 2 weeks.

Hot and sour mayo

YIELD 300ML (½ PINT)

175ml (6fl oz) good-quality mayonnaise

2 tbsp sour cream

2 tbsp Dijon mustard

2 tbsp white wine vinegar

¼ tsp dried red chilli flakes

1 garlic clove, crushed

Mix all the ingredients together in a bowl. The mayo is ready to use immediately but will keep well in the fridge, covered, for up to 1 week.

Green hot dog mustard

YIELD 300ML (½ PINT)

450g (1lb) green tomatoes, unpeeled and roughly chopped

1 onion, roughly chopped

2 green peppers, halved, deseeded and roughly chopped

½ cucumber, halved lengthways, deseeded and roughly chopped

2 tsp sea salt

50g (1¾oz) pickling spice

1 garlic clove, crushed

350ml (12fl oz) white wine vinegar

200g (7oz) demerara sugar

Combine the vegetables in a bowl, sprinkle with the salt and leave for 1 hour to draw out the excess water. Squeeze any remaining moisture out between the palms of your hands and place the vegetables in a blender with the remaining ingredients. Blitz to a coarse purée. Transfer to a pan and slowly bring to the boil. Reduce the heat and simmer for 20–25 minutes, until the mixture reduces and becomes syrupy. Leave to cool, then transfer to storage jars. Ideally leave for 2–3 days before eating to allow the flavours to develop. This will keep well in the fridge, covered, for up to 2 weeks.

Making a simple pan gravy

Making a well-flavoured pan gravy to serve with simple fried or roasted sausages is really easy. It doesn't take long and the results are always flavourful. Here are my tips:

1 Whichever way you've cooked your sausages, whether in a pan on the stove or in a roasting tin in the oven, make sure you keep the fat and juices left in the pan to start your gravy off.

2 You'll also need some stock. Ideally, use home-made stock, but stock cubes work nearly as well.

3 If you've cooked your sausages in a pan, remove with a slotted spoon, transfer to a plate and cover with tinfoil to keep warm while you prepare the gravy. If you've cooked them in the oven, simply reduce the oven temperature.

Below are a few of my favourite pan gravies. They all work well with any variety of sausage.

Red onion pan gravy

Fry 3 sliced onions until golden in the fat left from cooking the sausages. Add 1 tbsp of caster sugar and cook until the onions are caramelised. Pour over 75ml (3fl oz) of balsamic vinegar and 100ml (3½fl oz) of good red wine. Boil together for 2–3 minutes, then add 300ml (½ pint) of beef or chicken stock. Reduce the heat and simmer for 8–10 minutes, until the liquid has reduced by two-thirds. Whisk in 1 tbsp of redcurrant jelly and allow to melt. Season with salt and pepper to taste, then pour over the sausages.

Wine pan gravy

Follow the recipe for Red onion pan gravy, but replace the red wine with white wine, cider or a fortified wine such as port, Madeira or Marsala. These add richness and a natural sweetness to the finished gravy.

Herb-infused pan gravy

Follow the recipe for Red onion pan gravy, but add 1 tbsp of your favourite herb to the onions and replace the red wine with white. Strain the gravy before serving.

Condiment-infused pan gravy

Follow the recipe for Red onion pan gravy, but add 1 tbsp of prepared English or Dijon mustard to the finished sauce. You can strain the gravy before serving or leave the onions in it if you prefer.

Index

Resources

USEFUL WEBSITES
For advice, information and recipes

www.lets-make-sausage.com
www.lovepork.co.uk (home of the British Sausage Appreciation Society)
www.sausagemania.com

SAUSAGE-MAKING AND INGREDIENT SPECIALISTS
www.designasausage.com
www.kenwoodworld.com
www.magimix.com
www.sausagemaker.com
www.sausagemaking.org
www.weschenfelder.co.uk

Many leading department stores also sell kitchen equipment with sausage-making accessories.

SAUSAGE SHOPS AND TRADITIONAL BUTCHERS
Below are some of my favourite shops and butchers, selling great sausages either across the counter or online.

ALLENS OF MAYFAIR
A favourite London butcher selling award-winning sausages
www.allensofmayfair.co.uk
Tel: 0844 880 2460

BIGGLES GOURMET SAUSAGES
Specialist in gluten-free sausages in London
www.ebiggles.co.uk
Tel: 020 7224 5937

THE BRISTOL SAUSAGE SHOP
Fine gourmet sausage selection in Bristol
www.bristolsausageshop.co.uk
Tel: 0781 747 8302

COWMAN'S FAMOUS SAUSAGE SHOP
Lancashire family butchers for over five generations in Clitheroe
www.cowmans.co.uk
Tel: 0120 042 3842

CROMBIES OF EDINBURGH
Established over 50 years; great sausages for sale online
www.sausages.co.uk
Tel: 0131 557 0111

THE GINGER PIG
Award-winning sausage-maker with shops all over London
www.thegingerpig.co.uk
Tel: 01751 460 091

KETTYLE QUALITY MEATS
Top-quality meats and sausages
Tel: 020 7622 7101

MASHAM SAUSAGE SHOP
Award-winning family butchers in Ripon, North Yorkshire
www.mashamsausages.com
Tel: 0176 564 0009

M MOEN & SONS
Traditional award-winning family butcher
www.moen.co.uk
Tel: 020 7622 1624

SIMPLY REAL SAUSAGES
Offering over 40 great varieties
www.simplyrealsausages.co.uk
Tel: 020 7394 7776

SPECIALIST SAUSAGE MAKERS
BRINDISA
Great Spanish sausages
www.brindisa.com

CAMISA
Italian deli selling cured and fresh Italian sausages
www.camisa.co.uk
Tel: 0199 276 3076

THE BURY BLACK PUDDING COMPANY Terrific black pudding
www.buryblackpuddings.co.uk
Tel: 0161 797 0689

Author's acknowledgements

I have absolutely loved writing about sausages – one of the world's greatest comfort foods. As always when you write a book, there's a whole team behind the finished product, and this book is no exception.

Thanks go to **Jacqui Small** and **Kerenza Swift**, for their faith in the book and their guidance and support in its production from the first ideas to completion.

Thanks too to **Penny Stock**, for her beautiful book design.

To **Hilary Mandleberg**, the book's editor. Hilary, you have been an absolute pleasure to work with. Thank you so much.

To **Annie Rigg**, the home economist and **Will Heap** the photographer, thanks for making sausages look sexy! That's no easy feat!

Thanks to my chef team at **The Lanesborough Hotel**, especially **Callum Graham**, for his help in testing the recipes.

Finally my biggest thank you goes to my good friend, **Thierry Chenier**, master butcher of **Kettyle Quality Meats** for his generous help in getting together the sausage ingredients.

A truly big thank you to you all!

Publisher's acknowledgements

Thanks go to **Kenwood** for the loan of the Kenwood KM010 Titanium Chef featured on pages 24 and 25; to **Magimix** for the loan of the Magimix 5200XL, featured on page 24; and to **W Weschenfelder & Sons** for the loan of the Classic No.10 stainless steel manual mincer featured on page 24 and the Mini Plus Little Demon stuffing machine featured on page 26.